Jamie and Bess or the laird in disguise, a Scots pastoral comedy. In imitation of The gentle shepherd. By Andrew Shirrefs A.M.

Andrew Shirrefs

PRINT EDITIONS

Jamie and Bess or the laird in disguise, a Scots pastoral comedy. In imitation of The gentle shepherd. By Andrew Shirrefs A.M.

Shirrefs, Andrew
ESTCID: T029044
Reproduction from British Library

Aberdeen : printed and sold by the author, 1787.
x,[2],88,[4]p. ; 8°

Eighteenth Century
Collections Online
Print Editions

Gale ECCO Print Editions

Relive history with *Eighteenth Century Collections Online*, now available in print for the independent historian and collector. This series includes the most significant English-language and foreign-language works printed in Great Britain during the eighteenth century, and is organized in seven different subject areas including literature and language; medicine, science, and technology; and religion and philosophy. The collection also includes thousands of important works from the Americas.

The eighteenth century has been called "The Age of Enlightenment." It was a period of rapid advance in print culture and publishing, in world exploration, and in the rapid growth of science and technology – all of which had a profound impact on the political and cultural landscape. At the end of the century the American Revolution, French Revolution and Industrial Revolution, perhaps three of the most significant events in modern history, set in motion developments that eventually dominated world political, economic, and social life.

In a groundbreaking effort, Gale initiated a revolution of its own: digitization of epic proportions to preserve these invaluable works in the largest online archive of its kind. Contributions from major world libraries constitute over 175,000 original printed works. Scanned images of the actual pages, rather than transcriptions, recreate the works *as they first appeared.*

Now for the first time, these high-quality digital scans of original works are available via print-on-demand, making them readily accessible to libraries, students, independent scholars, and readers of all ages.

For our initial release we have created seven robust collections to form one the world's most comprehensive catalogs of 18th century works.

Initial Gale ECCO Print Editions collections include:

History and Geography
Rich in titles on English life and social history, this collection spans the world as it was known to eighteenth-century historians and explorers. Titles include a wealth of travel accounts and diaries, histories of nations from throughout the world, and maps and charts of a world that was still being discovered. Students of the War of American Independence will find fascinating accounts from the British side of conflict.

Social Science

Delve into what it was like to live during the eighteenth century by reading the first-hand accounts of everyday people, including city dwellers and farmers, businessmen and bankers, artisans and merchants, artists and their patrons, politicians and their constituents. Original texts make the American, French, and Industrial revolutions vividly contemporary.

Medicine, Science and Technology

Medical theory and practice of the 1700s developed rapidly, as is evidenced by the extensive collection, which includes descriptions of diseases, their conditions, and treatments. Books on science and technology, agriculture, military technology, natural philosophy, even cookbooks, are all contained here.

Literature and Language

Western literary study flows out of eighteenth-century works by Alexander Pope, Daniel Defoe, Henry Fielding, Frances Burney, Denis Diderot, Johann Gottfried Herder, Johann Wolfgang von Goethe, and others. Experience the birth of the modern novel, or compare the development of language using dictionaries and grammar discourses.

Religion and Philosophy

The Age of Enlightenment profoundly enriched religious and philosophical understanding and continues to influence present-day thinking. Works collected here include masterpieces by David Hume, Immanuel Kant, and Jean-Jacques Rousseau, as well as religious sermons and moral debates on the issues of the day, such as the slave trade. The Age of Reason saw conflict between Protestantism and Catholicism transformed into one between faith and logic -- a debate that continues in the twenty-first century.

Law and Reference

This collection reveals the history of English common law and Empire law in a vastly changing world of British expansion. Dominating the legal field is the *Commentaries of the Law of England* by Sir William Blackstone, which first appeared in 1765. Reference works such as almanacs and catalogues continue to educate us by revealing the day-to-day workings of society.

Fine Arts

The eighteenth-century fascination with Greek and Roman antiquity followed the systematic excavation of the ruins at Pompeii and Herculaneum in southern Italy; and after 1750 a neoclassical style dominated all artistic fields. The titles here trace developments in mostly English-language works on painting, sculpture, architecture, music, theater, and other disciplines. Instructional works on musical instruments, catalogs of art objects, comic operas, and more are also included.

The BiblioLife Network

This project was made possible in part by the BiblioLife Network (BLN), a project aimed at addressing some of the huge challenges facing book preservationists around the world. The BLN includes libraries, library networks, archives, subject matter experts, online communities and library service providers. We believe every book ever published should be available as a high-quality print reproduction; printed on-demand anywhere in the world. This insures the ongoing accessibility of the content and helps generate sustainable revenue for the libraries and organizations that work to preserve these important materials.

The following book is in the "public domain" and represents an authentic reproduction of the text as printed by the original publisher. While we have attempted to accurately maintain the integrity of the original work, there are sometimes problems with the original work or the micro-film from which the books were digitized. This can result in minor errors in reproduction. Possible imperfections include missing and blurred pages, poor pictures, markings and other reproduction issues beyond our control. Because this work is culturally important, we have made it available as part of our commitment to protecting, preserving, and promoting the world's literature.

GUIDE TO FOLD-OUTS MAPS and OVERSIZED IMAGES

The book you are reading was digitized from microfilm captured over the past thirty to forty years. Years after the creation of the original microfilm, the book was converted to digital files and made available in an online database.

In an online database, page images do not need to conform to the size restrictions found in a printed book. When converting these images back into a printed bound book, the page sizes are standardized in ways that maintain the detail of the original. For large images, such as fold-out maps, the original page image is split into two or more pages

Guidelines used to determine how to split the page image follows:

• Some images are split vertically; large images require vertical and horizontal splits.
• For horizontal splits, the content is split left to right.
• For vertical splits, the content is split from top to bottom.
• For both vertical and horizontal splits, the image is processed from top left to bottom right.

JAMIE AND BESS,

OR

The Laird in Difguife,

A

SCOTS

PASTORAL COMEDY,

IN

IMITATION OF THE

GENTLE SHEPHERD.

By ANDREW SHIRREFS A. M.

O rus, quando ego te afpiciam? quandoque licebit,
Nunc Veterum libris, nunc fomno et inertib s horis,
Ducere folicitæ jucunda oblivia vitæ?

Hor. Sat. VI. Lib. II.

ABERDEEN:

PRINTED AND SOLD BY THE AUTHOR.

M,DCC,LXXXVII,

(Price 1s. 6d)

ENTERED IN *STATIONER's HALL.*

N. B. Here is *Engravers* of the *Engravers*,
The OVERTURE *composed by the Author*,
of the *Leu*, *and the Songs in* SCORE, *price*
to *be given* FIVE *SHILLINGS.*

To The HONOURABLE The COUNTY CLUB of ABERDEEN-SHIRE.

My Lords and Gentlemen,

AS the Members of the CALEDONIAN HUNT condescended to patronize an Ayr-shire BARD, I was encouraged to hope, that The Noblemen and Gentlemen of the County of Aberdeen (who are inferior to none, in any thing which can render a man respectable) would vouch safe their generous patronage to a like humble BARD whose revenue, and property ever will be, without the limits of their counties, or who glories in the cultivation, of being acknowledged as their own.

The Performance, My Lords and Gentlemen, which I here respectfully infer be to you is of a part in some measure, had the fortune of the Public favour, in the approbation, with which it has been received, when exhibited repeatedly, on the Theatres, of Aberdeen. Elgin, and Invernels. But it is your defence the practice, among Poets and Writers in all ages, to choose some honourable Patron, to screen themselves and their productions, from the envy attacks of Ignorance and Envy. The propriety or impropriety of such choice, is a matter of a certainly unto often contingencies, of which, in the true regard being had to the nature of the Performance and the taste, or supposed character, of the intended Patron. Had my Performance been written in the most elegant and polished language and one of just deserving of attention, from the most learned or philosophic minds, it could never be accorded to none, with more propriety than to you Lords of that Patriotic spirit, which you there, from your illustrious ancestors whatever you have on many occasions, so eminently discharged would properly dispose you to favour a Performance, written in the Scots Dialect, and intended to convey a faithful, to

humble

humble, *and perhaps* weak *picture of the simple man-*
ners of the inhabitants *of your* native *Country.*

To you therefore, My Lords and Gentlemen, I
offer, as an humble tribute of y Esteem *and* respect,
the manners of my homely Muse. *And, tho'* my hopes
... a game, *I am animated by the* honour of
y ... influence *and* Patronage ... expect that my future ... disregarded. *If my present attempt is*
... your approbation *may I not flatter my-*
self ... to ... thought that my fortune (which has,
... worn out a sullen aspect,) *may yet, per-*
haps, put on a cheering *smile? And if, at any*
future ... I ... hope to make a more con-
... figure in the *literary* world, I will look ta-
... you, My Lords *and* Gentlemen, with an eye of
great ... *as the* GUARDIANS (*under* Heaven) *of my*
... *and as the* benignant CONSTELLATION,
... beamed the first friendly ray of light on my
Obscurity,

I have the honour to be, with the most profound *respect,*

My LORDS *and* GENTLEMEN,

Your Most *Obedient,*

Most *Humble, and*

Devoted Servant;

ANDREW SHIRREFS

Aberdeen,
Dec 7th, 1787;

To The CRITICS.

YE snarl'n' Critics, spare your bang,
  It s nae for you I write my Sang,
Sae fteek your gab, for ye'll be wrang,
            To think to teale me ;
Ere I reply, ye'fe a' ga'e hang,
            Think ye, I'll p'eafe ye?

I ken your aim, nae man ye want',
But get fool chiels again to chant,
That ye may fhak' your crap, ne'er fcant
            O' foul-mou'd win',
But, troth, wi' me (I ken your cant)
            Ye'll come ahin

Reply! na, na, I'll fee you firft,
Tho' ye, wi' rage, be like to burft,
Wi' guid brown ale I'd quench my thirft,
            An'l let ye be,
As lang's my boddom keeps the firft,
            Nae fear o' me.

I ken the warst ye're fit to say,
Is that I'm *Lime*---is that news?---heh!
That's been my case this mony a day,
    I ken o'er well,
And, therefore, I'm less fit for *Play*,
    Than *abler* chiel.

Yet, after a' I've said and dane,
Gin ye're resolv'd to clear my een,
Sae do, ye winna brak' a bane,
    I dinna fear ye;
Without anes jeein' number ane,
    Troth, I can hear ye.

Tho' ye sud deave me wi' your clatter,
Thinking to keep me in het water,
Ae word, again, I winna chatter,
    It sall be true.
I'll use nae weapon, but my *batter* †
    To slap your mou'.

Or else, mayhap, my *belel rung*, *
A' I that never yet was dung,
Which, nittled anes, I use, clean sing,
    A ro' my Foes,
May lay your vile ill-scrapit tongue,
    And flat your nose.

             But

† The Author is a Bookbinder to Trade
* The author (for several years, has been depriv'd of the
use of his Legs, and reduced to the necessity of using Crutches.

But, ere that I my humour tyn,
Twa moons into the lift full hie,
A third chiel too, gin ye incline,
    I' the mick a' ld'n,'
Sae keep your clack, gin ye 'e a min',
    And do my biddin'.

And gin ye do, I'se tell ye plain,
(Nae doubt, the speech will mak' ye fain,
It comes frae heart, as well as brain,
    At time maist handy,)
Your's with esteem, I will remain
    While CRIPLE ANDY.

INVOCATION

TO

ALLAN RAMSAY.

O! honeſt Allan, reſt you, ſaul,
  For mony a ſonny tale ye taul,
Forgi'e me, gin I be a baul',
           As ape your tune·
And lend me, for a while, your Call,
         'Till I be dane.

And. tho' ye think I wad abuſe it,
Yet, dinna cankerd'y refuſe it,
But, kindly, tell me, how to uſe it,
         And there's nae fear,
But I, in time, may lear to teaſe it,
        I ha e'ſome ear.

Nae that I think, by ony means,
I e'er will play ſe winſome tunes,
As you, or Scota s deareſt frien's,
        O' niceſt ſkill,
But, gin ye ll, kindly, try me anes,
        I ſe ſha' my *will*.
The beſt nown ſpi'l, afore they ſpin,
And tho' at firſt, I mak but din,
Gin anes ye pi. me in a fin,
        I'm but a youth,

And

And may, wi' pains, lear to ha'l in,

         An' bla' mair fmooth.

At firft, he frown'd, and fud right fnel'y,

It's grite prefumption, lat me tell ye,

Ye bla' my whiftle ! It wad fell ye,

         Ye hinna breath;

I lat you ha'e't, a while ! Na, yelly,

         I wad be laith.

Tho' I ha'e lent it aft before,

To Beattie, Rofs, and eke fome more,

Who, cannily, cud ftop ilk bore,

         And tightly fit it ;

Ye only wad difgrace the Core,

         Were ye ad'n ttit.

Yet, gin I thought that ye were fit,

Or that ye had ha'f fmergh or wit.

Says I—O! dinna lat me fit,

         And die for langer,

But try, firft, how I'll manage it,

         Syn fha' your anger

Well, tak' it, fays he, then, and try,

I ga'e a toot, and gar't it cry,

But a' the time, that he ftood by,

         I fhook for fear;

Says he, I fee ye ken the wy,

         Ye'll, maybe, lear.

This ga'e fome heart, I blew mair plain,

He cock'd his lugs, and I was fun

To hear him say, ye'll try't again,
    But flick —nae rinning,
To bla' o'er lang, but hurts the brain,
    At the beginning.
I wi't ye keep it for a wee,
And come, some ither time, and fee,
Gin ye're worth ony help frae me,
    Or prove defervin',
I jook'd as low as low cud be,
    And faid your fervan'.
Nor ha'e I feen him mair fin'fyn,
But I wad gi'e a pint o' wine,
Tho' I be poor, that I cud fhine,
    Or pleafure gi'e him,
In cafe, the whiftle I may tyn,
    When next I fee him.
O' cud I play in time and tune,
And finger right, ere he come roun',
Tho' fhabby now, and far laid down,
    I mith turn fatter,
And, maybe, rife and get aboon
    The broken water.
But, yet, nae for't gin I'm fnuff'd,
By Fortune I hae lang been buff'd,
I kenna how the Queen's fae huff'd,
    But I'm fair fkelpit,
And gin I maun be rougher cuff'd,
    I canna help it.

R O L O G U E

Written, and Spoken, by Mr SUTHERLAND.

IN days of *yore*, when proverbs rife had been,
   'Mongst others, there was one for Aberdeen,
The adage this, "*Aye, tak' your word again*"
From whence some wicked wits would fain imply
A double meaning couch'd, and fly cry,
Whene'er they find the time or cause convene,
"*Hoot man at a' you'll tak' your word again*"
To dash their gibes, one fact I'll tell alone,
"Mark, now, how plain a tale shall set them down"
A mer chant once, who liv'd in Aberdeen,
And kept a shop somewhere about the Green,
'To London City, yearly, made resort,
With stockings, shoes—and got good profit for't,
But chanc'd, one time, of money to fall short
As paper credit then was ever us'd,
And honest carl was loath to be refus'd,
The goods he bargain'd for he bluntly cry'd,
"I dinna like to take and be denny'd,
"What maun I do, gudeman? the siller's slack,
"Maun I gi'e up your goods, and gang back?
"Na" said the factor, "friend, since that's the case,
"And I like your good, old, honest face,
"Tak' home the goods, and when you come next year,
"To buy again, I trust you'll make all clear"
The time came round, then merchant paid the claim,
"Aye," quoth the Cit, "I'll take your word again"

   Now for our *Author* call'd I ween,
He was the president of his Sc ,
It to your favour he shall justly turn,
He'll boldly hope "*You'll take HIS word again*"

THE PERSONS.

M E N.

Sir ARCHIBALD	Mr Sutherland
JAMIE *in love with Pess*	Mr Tingey
SIMON *in love with Kattie.*	Mr Newbound
GEORDY *and* } *two Clowns.*	Mrs Tingey
NED }	Mr Biggs
DORY *Father to Kattie*	Mr Ross
BRANKY *Father to Simon.*	Mr Maclaren

W O M E N.

BESS.	{ *Supposed Neice of He-len, and taken into the Knight's service* }	Mrs Hamilton
KATTIE.	*Dory's Daughter.*	Mrs Sutherland
HELEN	{ *Sister-in law to Do-ry, and supposed Aunt of Bess* }	Mrs Newbound
CATHARINE	*Mother to Geordy*	Mrs Cuthell

SCENE, A Shepherd's Village and fields, some miles North-west of Aberdeen.

Time of Action, Within TWELVE HOURS.

JAMIE AND BESS.

ACT I. SCENE I.

PROLOGUE TO THE SCENE

The Ploughman dights to still the team,
And low of herds, while grazing at,
Bess to th' shepherd's t
Pleas'd with the prospect Nature yields,
Here, Dorysts and curious fields;
His first a rising-ground
Now, o' th' fields for a age,
It's pen just rise g to her f,
Rest her forward le
When wearing by thy street
E j it and your y fee hin ri,
Wi' joy, som of the frien

A Y honeft billy, are ye here fae feen,
Ye him a bidden hing at Aberdeen,
I thought ye'd be a a a month at leaft,
Folks dinna ay get fau'ts fae foon redref'd

Branky And maybe, niebour, that's the gate wi' me,
Whit ither ta'ken 'bout me can ye fae?

       B.   Be int,

Bethe, gen I had been mair lucky frien',
Ye wou'na fee me ftanding here alane.

Weel do ye ken, when matters a' were right,
I was'a to ha'e my brain in my fight.

Pat, nae, nae mair that pleafure will I boaft,
Since, fire, to me he is forever loft

I'm here again wairfe than I gaed awa,
I even had hopes, but now I've tint them a'.

Dor Ah B . . . ye're ay ready wi' your joke,
But this Alfra, briks, ye are come to mock

To lofe your jefts, I'm fure that's nae the cafe ;
I read fome better things i' your face

Whate'er the caufe, that Simon ifn't here,
I canna fay, but of ae thing I'm fear,

Gin it were true, that ye've fae haplefs been,
I'd warra't, ha ye wadna look fae green

. . . . I've got another caft
. . . . had, when we fa . . ither laft.

. . . . appea,
. . . .

Nae will . . . . lat clear be deen,
Ye . . . . fear, wha ghad has hearts than are.

For, tho' ye . . . . . . gineft art employ,
That . . . . . . fee o' your . . etrays your joy,

Pra . . ce, the, Dog, it's but vain to try
To hide the joy, which e'e fo clearly fo,

I . . . . t on I'll tint my plea,
But ye're o . . . . and for t . . . . . . that to doe

'Tis as ye think, I'm free of a' my pain,
And my loo'd chiel is, now, anes man, my ain
See, gin affairs fall gae no farer wrang,
He fall be Dory's too, ere it be lang,

   Dor. Wi' a' my heart, I wis' it were he might,
Gin matters cud, fae foon, be gotten right
To, trow me, Branky, I'm as weel as glad,
As Kate herfell, wha is to ha'e the lad
Whare ha'e ye left him, that he na here,
If ain wad ken, and how ye gat him clear?
But, 'twill be better, now, to keep the wit,
Till we have gane and cas'd poor Kate's heart
The news, to her, will bring as grite relief,
As e'er reprieve did' to a fear'd thief

   Bra. Na, nibour, but ye need na fafte or head,
O' fic relief Kate difna far in need
Believe me frien', ye ha'e nae news to tell,
She kent the matter, ere ye wat yourfell
I met your lafs, as I was coming here,
And left my Simon and her doubts to clear
They baith forgether'd, to 'k, ' the wo'k,
And I fho' l aff and l ft them to their ow'k

   Dor. Nae mifs o' that, fae lang I ween,
They'll nae be angry they are left alane
Atweefh themfe'ls there b l can tale the pain,
Lovers have ay fome clatter o' their ain
I'll warrant nibour, when we woo'd our fell,
We didna like ilk ane fud hear our tale.

Nae third and person sud be near,
Love's tales are only for the Lover's ear
I own 'tis right, tho' it's o'er aften done,
To mak' love motions in a place unseen;
Meek to ear' leanings of a min'
Whats ow' obstacles, or wi' waise design,
I ve tel me man' own matters were agreed,
(i by whas intreat ye gat Simon freed ?

    Bes. And wha weil cud, the *Provost o' the town* ;
A jelly man, well worthy of a crown.
To him I gaed as soon's I reach'd the place,
By frien's advice, to lat him ken my case ,
And tho' grite folks are sometimes unco' shy,
And speak right four to sic as you or I ;
He kindly heard my story to an end,
And syn he straight did for the sergeant send,
Wi' pointed word to bring my son alang,
That he mith ken wha's tale was right or wrang.
Syn, in a short, my blustrin' blade appears,
And he a hunder questions at him spiers :
To some of which he meant but sma' reply,
But boot to gi'e a *wherefore* for ilk *why*.
Nor durst ae word he spake be out o' joint,
But a', he said, boot just be to the point.
For tho' he play'd the Lord into the fair,
Nought but submissive speech cud answer there.
'Twas easy dare, to fright plain fouks like we,
But yon er, faith, he fan it wadna doe.

In fhort, my fri'd', on a' thing was brought out,
My boy was clear'd, and enn'd to the boot,
A guid round fum, a twenty fhillings note,
Nor wad his Honour pafs ne fingle groat

Dor Ye chear my heart—how was the billy pleas'd,
Nae well, I wad, to be fo fnelly us'd?

Bra. O had ye feen, wi' what a waefu' frown,
He drew lang-craig and taull the fcufhy down,
I'm fure, ye cudna fee a queerer fight,
His very vifage was amaift a fright
As lang's I live, I'll laugh ay, when I think,
Wi' what a waefu' phiz he twinn'd his clink.

Dor Troth, nibour, and ye ay may blifs him for't,
Who was the caufe o' fic a hearty fport.
He cuda gart you fing anither tune,
Ye've been mair lucky, footh, than mony ane.
For grant ye had a' juftice in your caufe,
Yet innocence whiles fuffers by the laws.
Some judges dinna gi'e decrees fae juft,
He's been a man well worthy o' his truft.
Some wadna ta'en fic pains to get the truth,
But, right or wrang, wad let him keep the youth,
Or gart you craw, afore ye gat him clear,
Mair frae your purfe, than it cud rightly bear.

Bra. Things as unjuft by judges ha'e been dane,
But never think 'twas fae at Aberdeen.
Ye manna fpeak o' them in fic a ftrain,
They've ay been kent for downright honeft men;

Wha's

Wha's ilka action speer is the r grown' fame,
And shew them justice, worth o' the name
By dem the l gie no regard yet,
Guilt is the cry, object of men hate,
To punish when they use the greatest art,
But never, never, act a unjust part

Pa. We'll come my frien', whatever be the case,
We'll drink the cap, in honour of the place,
And drink his health, wha set our Simon free,
At ha merry meeting 'till we die.

                    [*Exeunt.*

SCENE II.

PROLOGUE TO THE SCENE

*The ba's, at least, may please your ee,
O what y're, now, about to see,
A, de, a wee bit frae the ma'k,
'Bout what ye heard auld Brachy crack.
True a', but you, birk bushes hide,
Twa lovers seated, side by side,
       Upon a flowery bank,
The twa are Simon and his Kate,
Nor wonder tho' the laa looks blate,
       As us'd o' sic a prank
I've left his lass ye heard afore,
You, hear them flyte upon the score,
       But then ye needna fear,
Tho' she maun ha'd him out o' langer,
Love lurks beneath her seeming anger,
       And u'ere lang appear*

SANG

S A N G I

Tune——*Sorry o'er the Lee*

My S...... ....,
　'That's ...th.ng fear,
But it had better been,
　Had he been w..e,
　And ta'en advice,
I ne'er f.. days had feen

　Some figh'ng faid,
　'I'o' they were glad,
We're wae we've t.nt your lad
　"I is hard that he,
　Sud take .ore thee,
A faxpence and cockade.

　Since, firft, he fled,
　'Ine life I've led,
Has been a life o' pain.
　Some jeer'd me fair,
　A' cry'd nae mair,
Will he return ag. n

S I M O N

　Ne'er mind their crack,
　Now I'm come back,
Let inward pining ceafe,
　My folly paft,
　May be the laft,
'That e'er will brak' your peace.

Ka.

Ka. But tell me, Simon, now that ye are free,
How cud you tak' sae little thought o' me?
Gin Kate had, anes, but enter'd i' your head,
Ye never cud ha'e dane sae rash a deed.

Sm Kate may believe, altho' I didna tell,
When that was dane, I wasna just mysell
Yet tho' mischance led me to play the fool,
My heart, to her, was ever true and leal
She was my thought, while I had pow'r to think,
But ilka thought that's guid is drown'd by drink.

Ka Ah Simon, troth, that's but a blate excuse,
Whase faut was it your head was i' the bees?
'Twas i' your pow'r to lat the drink alane,
Or drink, in measure, and there's sma' ill dane.
I wadna lat the trash come near my mou',
That e'er wad drown sae sweet a thought as you

Sm. Ere ye condemn me, hear me plead my cause,
That's, sure, allow'd by Love's severest laws.
Anes ye have heard the truth o' the affair,
Maybe ye mayna blame me ha'f sae far.
When I set out, I meant to spend my cunk,
On something ither than a drap o' drink
Ere I gaed there, I was a happy man,
Friends had agreed I su'd ha'e Katty's hand.
Fou o' the hopes of this my prom's'd joy,
I sought the Fair, for ither the employ,

To

To coff what bonny trinkets I mith fee,
By way o' fairin' to my lafs, fae me
Nae harm, tho' I ha'e brought her ane or twa,

                              [*Prefenting her a' fome*

Sic bonny trocks to help to mak her bra.
I'ddna mean to pit a' down my throat,
Nor maun my Katty think fhe was forgot.
E'en when I drank till I was piper fu',
The very caufe, my Katty, it was you.
As I was coffin' at my trinkets there,
I met a frien or twa into the Fair,
Wha kent the happinefs I had in view,
And they booth ha'e mean to fee my dew.
When we were fet, your health gaed firft o'a',
And ilk ane, there, drank to his bricer or,
Syn kifs'd it's boddom, as a fmack fu' fmart,
To fhaw your weal lay deep within his heart.
Say then, my Katty, was't a richt reboot,
Was I to be beholder of a' this
When a' grew wanton in my favour fo,
And wifh'd her mickle bewty and her joys,
Could I fyn flight her and his toil to fee,
Or fhaw myfelf fo by her tongue fo?
   Ka. It's true, ne doubt, for me to own it too,
E'en of the beft, who proued fo fou,
Bat what's o' gude ane reckon'd, though,
Bat her return to her when fhe will,
Gae to fome market there about or fell
O Kate or banes, that fhe can't mak'd fae.

                                                I

I ken my Simon has o'er mickle sense,
When he is sober, e'er to gi'e offence.
We'e he ay so, he then wad ay be kind,
But then, anither tout may change his mind
Where drink gets in, baith wit and sense flee out,
And he mith may be ta'en anither rout.
Syn whare is Kate, when her Simon's gane,
But left to mis'ry, may be nae alane.
How can ye think, I ever wad agree,
To tak' a man, that may forhou me ?
But, sud ye stay at hame and stick by Kate,
Her sorrows maybe nith be just as great.
A drunken man's the hinder-end of a',
What tho' my Simon's bonny now and bra,
Gin he likes drink 'twad alter soon the case,
And drunken chapins blether a' his face.
It soon wad gar his love to me turn cauld,
And mak' him daz'd and doited ere half auld.
Drink's aft the cause o' muckle dool and strife,
And L is a' confort atween man and wife.

S—. Nae doubt when drinkin's carried to excess,
It's sure to blast the seeds of happiness,
And are that's drink wad aft commit a crime,
He'd fear to think of, ony ither time
Put who's sae strang as o'er to turn his grip,
Or who sae wise as never to aslip?
Tho' I hae anes transgress'd found reasons lar e,
Ye ken, my Kate, was in an hon'rous cause ,

And

And I ha'e suffer'd for't baith lang and fair,
Ye needna seek to mak' my sorrows mair.
Tho' I have been the caufe o' Katie's pain,
I dreed as mickle, fure, for her again
And Katty needfna mak' fae grite a phrafe
I's ne'er be fu', again in a' my days
Of a' my days to come it's be the care,
To mak' her juft as happy as fhe's fair

Ka. Gin Simon hates to lead a fingle life,
And gin he canna do without a wife,
Were it the fafhion to ha'e mair than are,
Gin he inclines, he needfna lie alane
He's ill beftead, wha canna pfs ae doon,
Twad mak' fma' odds tho' I fud gi'e him o e,
I'm very fear he wadna want a fcore,
O' laffes full as likely to the ee,
And handfomer, by mony fies, than me

Sim What I mith get, my Kate, is nae the thing
Ye fud be Queen, tho' Simon were a King
I mony a ftrappin' lafs, nae doubt ae fee,
For there's nae want of them About her
There's fcarce a laffie, there, that ye wad fee,
But wha has fomething in her face that's fweet
Ill the Town for Beauties it furpaffes,
It's juft the nurfery o' bonny laffes
Yet, tho' I've feen them a' and mony mair,
I ne'er faw ane, wi' Kate, that cud compare.
I ne'er faw a lafs in a' my life,
I'd mak' fae foon as bonny Kate my wife,

                                    Ka.

Ke. Well's my Simon how to touch my heart,
Will Ke's he how to act the Lover's part,
Can you as kindly act the Husband's too,
You'll ever find a loving wife in me.

SANG II

Tune—O my Bony, &c. Lillie &c

SIMON

WERE't not for Kate's too pow'rful charms,
I like the proud and lighter dress,
But ev'ry thought of war and arms,
I gladly quit for her embrace

KATTIE

O honey'd accents far too sweet,
They like enchantment to me seem,
My happiness is too complete,
Ah! Simon, sure, I only dream!

[*Falling into his arms.*

To what, shall I my bliss compare!
In Simon I have ev'ry wish—

[*Simon folding her in his arms.*

Then, in your bliss let Simon share,
And make him happy with a kiss

KATTIE

It kisses gi'e him sic relief,
I ha'e a treasure for his sake,
And never need he taste of grief,
Since at discretion, he may take.

SIMON

SIMON.

Far hence be ilk intruding care,
While thus I press thee to my breast,
Ten thousand sweets ye have to spare,
And ane to me, my Kate's a feast

KATTIE

Such kisses as I thus bestow,
I only to my Simon lend,
When sweeter on his lips they grow,
He'll, kindly pay them back again

SIMON

O' never can those sweets increase
Bestow'd like Nature s on the flow rs,
For what ye think my lips possess,
My Kattie only flows frae your s

KATTIE

If freely gie'n, with loving heart,
They sweeter be, then such are mine
But never can my lips impart,
A sweet not far excell'd by thine.

BOTH

Soon may the happy day appear,
When we may kiss, nor care wha ken't,
When greater bliss our hearts will share,
And we embrace without restraint.

ACT

ACT II. SCENE I.

PROLOGUE to the SCENE

To Cath'rine's dwalling, just hard by,
The Knight, &c., stepping in the way,
    Right spruse, wi' varnish'd care,
List what he says, he'll stay but short,
But mean to gi'e you better sport,
    When he comes back again

STRANGE news, indeed,—but Cath'rine comes
  And ere I speak, I better think a wee, [I see;
How, to best purpose, I may play my part;
I wish it dinna gae beyond my art.
I'm sure I'll find it a right trying task,
To act it a' beneath a serious mask.
Gin Geordy be the rattle-scull I'm taul,
I may expect to find him stiff and baul.
But I'll first see what Lucky says hersell,
Gin she can ought about this matter tell.
From what she says, I'll maybe guess the lave,
And get some notion how I maun behave.
I find the Carlin's ta'en anither tour,
I'll see to catch her, ere she win hame o'er.   [*Exit.*

SCENE II

PROLOGUE to the SCENE

Their backs supported by a tree,
  Twa lads in close discourse, ye see,
    Nae doubt, they'll friends appear,

                                But

But thinkna this, or ye're misſta'en,
Folks manna ay believe their een,
                    Nor credit a' they hear,
Sly Ned, ſic kindneſs but preterds,
Like mair, to anſwer his ain erds,
                    For he likes Geordy's laſs,
And kenſna how to ding in out,
But hopes to bring's intent about,
                    'Cauſe Georay's but an aſs

Ned. Well, I can tell you nowther man nor leſs,
But, gin ye're wiſe ye will keep clear o' Beis
She is a ſly and cunning quean I ken,
And wi' the Knight is rather o'er far ben.
From what I heard, within this little wee,
Her apron ſhortens to the ſkilly ce.
An honeſt curian, that ye l en fu well,
Taul' me, for certain, that ſhe is wi' ch el ,
And that ſhe'd lay, ere lang it wad be ſeen,
By fouks wha hinna juſt the cleareſt een

  Geo. That a , they ſay, and mickle mair is true,
I thought langſyn, but mony thanks to you
For o' your kindneſs, I il ne can think the leſs,
'That I afore kent what ye now expreſs
But fearna frien', as lang's the ſun may ſhine,
Into the lift ſhe never ſall be mine
I own I anes had liking for the yade,
But couk to think o't ſince ſhe turn'd a Lawd.
Ye manna think that I'm ſae big an aſs,
His Honour's leavings ne er ſall be my laſs.

                                                    Since

Since it is fae, I'll better try fome ither—

   Ned. Yet, I am taul' ye twa are aft thegither.
Now, gin ye wad be counfell'd by a frien,
Nae mair, again, be feen wi' her you lane.
Fouks that obferve,— or blame you unco fair,
Or think that ye ken nought o' the affair.
It wad be right to tell her, that ye ken
Her bonny pranks, and then ha'e fairly dane.

   Geo It's eafy lad, for you to fhaw the way,
To fhak aff laffes, gin ye come to try,
Ye'll find it's nae fo eafy brought about,
By the tae ha'f, as it is pointed out.
Anes lat a hiffy get you in the girn,
Ere ye get loofe, ye'll red a ravell'd pirn.
In ilk refpect, I've been as wife as ye,
Tried mony methods, but fan nane wad doe
Aft, when fhe fpak' I made her nae reply,
And, when I met her proudly whiftled by,
On ilk occafion, I ha'e fhawn neglect,
Dane a' I cud, and yet to nae effect

   Ned That's very ftrange indeed—I reckon,
Gin it were me, I fhortly fud be clear
Ye maun ha'e acted fomething man not right,
That gars her ftand fae out agains your might —

   Geo Laft night, I faw her, yon'er on the brae,
She wagg'd her hand and meant that I fud ftay.
But, when fhe faw fhe met wi' nae regard,
She fcauld, and cried, fhe vad inform the Laird

She said, she lang had suffer'd cau'd neglect,
But he wad gar me pay some mair respect.
Gin she has tauld, it shortly will appear,
He and my mither, see, are coming here
They seem right earnest, as they trudge along,
I'll warran't prove the burden o' their sang.
But, gin it do, their travel is in vain,
I'll never wed to lead a life o' pain.
I am resolv'd, ae word I canna tin,
If he but speak, I'll tell him plain my mind.

Ned Be as it may, ye shortly now will see,
But hear me, lad, I'll tell ye what to due.
Afore, ye lat him get o'er mickle time,
To shak' his crap and scaud you for the quean,
Be bauld enough to tell him a' your mind
Shaw how the hussy's us'd you saft and hard,
An' bauldly tell the cause of a' their spite.
But as ye'd wish to clear yourself o' blame,
Be sure, you dinna mention anes my name.

Geo Believe me, Ned, I've nae sic fool intent.
I'se pledge my troth, ye never sal be kent
Afore that I reward your friendliness sae,
The sun shall shine by night, the moon by day.
A'thing turn topsy-turvy in a trice,
Wise fouls turn fools, and fools turn wondrous wise
Ned I'll leave you, ther, and hie me to the fell,
St ck to your p int———   [E t.
Geo ——————————In nae respect I'll y——
                              SANG
                    D

SANG III

Tune—Hear and there &c.

THE reuſl in Beſs, for wny ſud I fear?
   Tho', nae doubt, my deſerd anes warmly did burn,
In nae feard as, as eam'd a laſs,
Wha o'trust ſoe er suck nder return

Tho De'l, &c, nau th' me, nae vows, ſure can bin' me,
To ſee her ſe l'f, m' a is a ſcand urkin',
Tae I n'v e her before, ro I hate her the more,
For g ng another wha ſud a been mine

It s my part to ſlight her, and his, ſure, to right her,
And a he beſ can he me, go h himſell
I lla'c my throat nicked, ere I nere fae tricket,
Or the wand, on me, gat fe ſtoras to te'

Had ſhe conſtant prov'd, I ſ I would have lo d
But ſlud s owerwi e I m nae to b ame,
I ſcorn the Beauty, who la th her cut,
And wiſhes to pa me the anng agare

Enter Carl'n r erl t'e Engl

Cath. I George! I ne er thought to ſire the day,
That folks of you, ſae muckle n' aa ſar,
Ah, fy for ſhame! to be ſa croſs to Beſs,
As force the Knight to come and ſeek rediets!
In truth c reall now, ma n g e your hand,
Ye'll be mair kind, ard p o e an ther man.

Geo. I'll tell you plain, g teling likes to doe
Nane need to come that e land reie tome.

                I ve

I've fhawn mair kindnefs than fhe's worthy o',
Or ony quean that cud ha' us'd re fo
   Kn. Some decency, young-man, ve muft obferve,
From you, fuch treatment, fhe coul ne er defarve.
Why not fulfill the promifes ve made?
Ye fought the lafs, and took ye ent it to wed
Nae farther kindnefs, now, for h   care,
Juftice is a' fhe feeks and that fhe ll have.
   Geo I o fe promife ore e tap'd y mou',
But, then, your Honour, fh was kent for true,
So, free whatever I mith fay 'efore,
I'm now fet free, fince fhe s g ne o' the fcore [hat?
   Kn Gane o'er the fcore! what mean ve youal, by
   Geo. I'm well informed, fhe's vr' a but   ab t
   Cath Bafe he indeed——
   Kn ——————————To whom does it ay peat?
   Geo It s to your Honour——
   Kn —————————————me!
   Geo ——————————————E en fae I fa
   Kn That fpeech, young man, ca eafh! frae y ur
But, ye'fe be free, gin ye can make it ut   friend,
Gin e'er I harm'd her, fae will fa y, + l,
Nane can know better than the lafs herfell.
She'll be brought to you, and fhe fha't declare,
What's truth or falfchood, now, in th   af
Gae Catharine for the lafs, and we fhall   ,
And gin fhe f ye't, I take her and ye'fe free

                                       But

But mind, young man, if it shall now appear,
Your Foy's tale and I am wholly clear,
Ye then, wi' Bels creaty maun agree,
Or elfe my just difp'eafure ye shall dree.

Geo I winna mak' fic bargains, fir, e'en now,
The lafs wad ha'e but fma' wit in her pow,
Gin fhe wad ftick to truth in fic a cafe,
And be the trumpet o' her ain difgrace.
I'l warran fhe cud mak' a fwingin' lie,
To patch up matters, gin fic things wad doe.
I never fail, by tricks, be cullied o'er,
To wed a lafs your Honour's us'd afore.
Ye needna think I am fae big a fool,
I ne'er will fwallow fic a bitter pill.

Cath Forgi'e him, fir, he's fure nae kenning right,
To whom he cracks Fine ufage to the knight !
His Honour, troth, may think you right ill bred,
Anes ye're at hame, I'fe gar your back be pay'd.

[*Strikes him with her staff.*

Geo My back be pay'd ! o' that I hinna fear,
And what his Honour thinks I fanna care.
Nae fatisfaction fair'er will I gi'e,
I plainly tell you Befs is nae for me

Cath Gae from my fight, ye worthlefs piece o' wark !
I'fe gar your father learn you how to bark !
Ye needna think fic faucy clack fall pafs,
Ye fall do war, gin ye'll nae wed the lafs !

Of

Of a the fons that I ha'e ever had,

Except yourfel, ilk ane has made me glad,

They never ta ild a laffie o' their love,

And fyn neglected, when fhe did approve.

Ill-manner'd dog! ye ve anger d me right fair,

Strikes him again

Swith frae my fight, nor lat me fee you mair!

An like your Honour, ye'll gang back wi' me,

I'll warran William gar him foon agree,

To tak the lafs, and mak' his promife guid,

Or elfe the rogue fal' claw a broken head

Kn Na, George, come back, and Cath'rine gae your

Ye are o er warm a pleader in this caufe.   [wa's

Force ne'er can do, that manna be the way,

He fall be fatisfied, ere he comply.

Geo. Well, gin it's poffible that can be dane,

I'll own my faut and hope to be forgi'en

Cath How can ye think his Honour will forgie,

Sic foul mou'd win frae fic a cur as ye?

Own that ye lied, and that his Honour's wrang'd,

Ere we re difgrac'd, and ye yourfell be hang d!

Kn Cath'rine now leave's, and we may chance to

Without or hanging him, or fhaming thee.   ['gree,

Cath. God blifs your Honour, ye may hear my mean,

I'll ne'er do guid, gin he meet fic an end!

Will am and I, I'm fure are nae to blame,

We ne'er heard ony blot upon your name.   *Exit*

Geo.

Geo Your Honour needsna ha'e a grudge at me,
There's mair, wha sud be hang'd, if that's a lie.
I'm nae the maker o' the tale I'se swear,
And he that tauld me ne'er was ca'd a liar.
Let gin your Honour thinks to prove him sae,
He sud be punish'd and I latten gae.
I'se only tauld you what I heard mysell,
And what ane hears I thought nae sin to tell

K. Tales that are good, or harmless, when ye hear,
You may, with freedom, spread them far and near
But lies, or tales, which blast your neighbour's fame,
Whoe'er spreads them surely, is to blame

Geo And I'll your Honour, gin it be true,
I neer tauld to ony ane but you,
And had I thought ye'd ta en't sae much amiss,
I had been sa plain as tell you this
I wad I een the tale wad hurt you sa r
For gentle fou k's thought o' the affair.
Anger'd at ane I think ye ha'e sma' reason,
Some souls, like you, think naething of a dizen
I've be angry, Bess may gae hate,
Gin ony's blam'd she's sure to get the wyte
Her it may hurt, what's ga'en, about upon her,
But fouk a man will ony think your Honour.

K. However base the opinion of the times,
It nae can make a virtue, sure, of crimes!
If there's a wretch, so destitute of shame,
So careless of his or and neighbour's fame,

As make himfelf the fcoff of fuch as thee,
He fhames mankind, whatever his degree ,
Forfeits a' rev'ience to his rank that's due,
And juftly ftands a monfter to the view !

Geo. Whatever monfters, fir, they may appear,
There are fic monfters, fa'at, I'm very fear.
And nae few o' them, either, as I ween,
They're in ilk ither corner to be feen
And this, I think, is far frae ony proof,
They're either heid as monfter, or as thief.
Nae doubt, when ony fic poor chiel as me,
Plays tricks, like that, ye'll in a hurry, fee
It, thro' the parifh, raife an unco' bree!
Sane as ane kens a lafs gets the gill-wheep,
Scandal's o'er guid a tale to fa' afleep
Whae ei was throngeft wi' the lafs before,
They lay the blame, for common, at his door.
This ane tells that, and that ane tells anither,
Nor wad they hoot't, on fler or on brither
Some wyte the lafs, ane where ane the lad,
And fae the ftory round about is ca'd,
Till fome auld Dad. mair haly than the reft,
Finds it his duty to acqu t the Prieft.
Syn there's nae help, but the poor lad maun ftand
Afore the kirk, to get a repri mand
And when they hae him frae the pu'pit taun,
How mickle, by the fir, he's hai d his faul ,

Ane

Ane fains herfell, anither granes a pray'r,
As gin he were the only finner there.
And ever after, he's ay pointed at,
As ane wha had, wi he a chiel, the brat.
Sae it fa's out, when poor fouks mifbehave,
They're juft made fcare-craws o' to a' the lave,
But, in a life time, now, ye winna hear,
Of ane fae roughly uf'd that ifna poor.
For gentle blades, wha have a fouth o' cafh,
To dit fouks mou's ne'er meet wi ony fafh.
However daft they wi the laffes be,
It s ay o'er-look'd, gin they but pay the fee.
Tho' gin they gat their due, I wat fu' well,
Ilk ither funday, fome wad fit the ftool.

_Kr._ Were they fae uf'd, it would be juft the fame,
Who cinna dread the fin, wou'd mock at fhame.
That wretch is loft who, fcaping cenfure here,
Of future punifhment betrays no fear!

Geo. I'm led to think, however ftrange to tell,
Sic canna trow there's ony place like Hell,
Or that to fic a pitch of vice thy're brought,
As gin there be or no ne'er cofts a thought.
But gin fome dinna, foon, their manners mend,
They'll fin't o'er true I'm fair fear'd in the end.
Nae that I mean your Honour, I'd be laith,
I e'er wad wifh ye meet fae mickle fkaith.
Tho' it fae be, that ye have fpoil'd my fport,
And I, nae doubt, am e'en right gut angry for't,

                                            Tho'

Tho' a' were true upon you I've been taul',
I wadna, for it a', ve'd lose your saul

 Kn. George, I still thought that ye had better sense,
Than use supe iors with such impudence
I never harm'd the lass in a' my life,
Else I wad never bid you call her wife
Ye've been o'er rash to credit sic a tale,
But gin ye tell your author, without fail,
Him I shall punish, and ye shall be free,
Either to take the lass, or lat her be

 Geo. Fairer than that, I'm sure, I cudna seek,
But then my tongue's boun' up, I dinena speak.
I've sworn nae to tell, ye maun excuse,
Gin I to answer your demand refuse.
Whaever taul' me, taul' me as a frien',
And to reveal him, sir, wad be ill dane.

 Kn. Well, George, I sanna bid you brake your troth,
Gin ye have sworn, man, ye may keep your oath.
But he, who taul' you, is nae friend to you,
And what I say, I ll shortly prove is true.
I'll find him out, altho' ye dinna tell,
If I should summons up auld *Nick* himsell.
But see, young-man, ye dinna tell a lie,
If a' the blame, at last, shall light on thee,

 Geo. Your Honour may do what ye like wi' me.
Whae'er I's ned, I was sae mayna pains,
May auld *Nick* get him for a baggage ass,

<table>
<tr><td>   E</td><td>To</td></tr>
</table>

To spur wi' red-het gauds thro' dub and mire,
And gar him carry a' his winter fire !

Kn And so he shall, nae better it shall be,
With him wha's found the author of this lie,
Unless that he appear, in proper time,
And own his fault and sorrow for the crime.
But gin I ra se the De'il, I'se plainly tell,
He winna' gae, without him back to Hell.
No i, gae to wark, but ere I sleep this night,
I'll shov you a' the matter brought to light.
Whae'er he be, I'll strive to make him feel

[*Exit George.*

As the KNIGHT turns about, enter BRANKY.

Bra. Goode'en, goode'en, I hope your Honour's well.

Kn I thank you Branky, what's the news in town ?
Pit on, pit on. How's Simon ?

Bra.————————Safe and sound
Thanks to your Honour for your friendly aid,
My chiel's my ain, and I am e'en right glad
Your kindly letter had a guid effect,
And gat me mickle kindness and respect
It pat the matter in sae clear a light
It wasna lang 'til we gat stories right;
And for the kindness as your Honour show'd,
I thought it but a duty, that we ow'd,
To come and thank you, foon as we gat hame,
But that we'd ane Branky's nae to blame.

To

'To mak' this poor acknowledgment we meant,
But as we're on the gratefu' errand bent,
We met 'wi' Beſſy, at her aunty's door,
Wha taul's ye ga'ed weſt-by a wee before.
This hour, ſays ſhe, ye mayna ſee his face,
Tho' ye ſud tramp it forward to the place
I'ſe lat you ken, as ſoon's I ſee him paſs,
But I wad, Simon rather ſee his laſs
Ye needna think to Stay, I'm very fear,
He'll ſit on nett'es a' the time he's here
And Kate, poor laſs, has need o' ſome relief,
She's juſt been like to fell herſell wi' grief
When this he heard, he wadna ba'd nor bin',
For fear that he mith maybe come al n,
But ſcour'd awa, as faſt as heels cud drive,
And happly fan' the laſs was ſtill alive

Kn. That a' is well, Branky, I'm mair than paid,
For ony trouble ye may think I had
Ye've been an honeſt tenant to me lang,
I would be laith to ſee you ſuffer wrong
Tho' it had coſt me ſomething mair than faſh,
I wadna grudg'd to ſpend a little caſh,
Ere Kate had loſt her lad, and ye your fon,
I wad have made them bear a greater din.

Bra God bliſs your Honour, ye was ever kind,
And a' that ken you, ken your genr'ous mind.
On ſic, as you, Heav'n's bounty's well beſtow'd,
May you, nor your's, ne'er want a fouth o' gowd.
                                        Nor

Nor are he scant, wi' sic an open heart,
O that, wi' which, he wad sae eithly part !

   Ka. To ease Oppression's load and make it light,
I lue to do our duty, and what's right.
Narrow's the saul, wha winna twin his gear,
To smooth misfortune's brow, or help the poor!
And mae the buddom o' his purse fa' out,
Wha has the pow'r, yet wants the will to do't :
Wha unconcern'd sees modest merit die,
For want o' what, unmiss'd, he cud supply!
For kinder purpo es, by bounteous Heaven,
Such superfluues to man are given,
And where bestow'd, it's plain they are design'd,
Not to contract, but to enlarge the mind.
For they're nae langer blessings than they're us'd,
They turn a curse, whene'er they are abus'd.
But where's your nephew, Branky? Is he here ?
I'll wad he's been of use gin ane may spier,
He is nae senseless lad, as I can see.

   Bra. He's far frae that, were he nae kin to me,
The lad, I can assure you did nae ill,
And twa three wonder'd how he had sic skill.
His clatter wadna sham'd an aulder man,
And I maun speak for him, now. gin I can.
The lad likes Bess, but Helen is sae proud,
She disna seem to think the bargain good.

   Ka. What wad she have ? I think the match is fair,
And that it e en sud answer to a hair !

                              Bra.

Bra. Some cantrip caſtin' cock, wha ſpells can read,
I underſtand has turn'd auld Lucky's head.
Her niece is bonny, and gin ſhe be ſpu'd,
She hopes to ſee her wedded to a Laird.

Kn. Sic wonders may, in former days, have been,
That Lairds have wedded laſſes full as mean.
I've ſeen when folks, for love, would ſometimes wed,
But marriage, now, is made a ſort of trade.
Wha bids the maiſt, is ſure to win the prize,
While ſhe that s tocherleſs neglected dies.
If ane be poor, and of a humble birth,
Whate er her merit be, whate'er her worth,
Wanting this ae commodity, the caſh,
A ither qualities are held but traſh.
Of matches, now o' days, ſuch is the mould,
Love rarely enters, but the love of gold.

Bra. Ay, true's the tale, and Helen needſna think,
Her niece will catch a Laird, without the clink.
There's few will marry ane without a groat,
Beauty alane will nae pit on the pot.
They've wanted a' their days, who were as bra,
She may be blyth to get a man ava ;
Or pitting grandeur freely out o' head,
Be mair than thankfu' to get ane that's guid.

Kn. But how ſtands Beſs ? Likes ſhe the lad herſell ?

Bra. Ay, wi' her ſaul, as far as I can ſmell.
And gin that Helen canna be brought too,
I kenna what the conſequence may be.

Kn.

Kn. Gin that be true, I'll gi'e the match a heeze,
And try to cure auld Helen o' the bees
For much I doubt, ye ken gin I be right,
She'll lose the Laird, gin she your nephew slight

Bra I watna, sr, how it cud come about,
That ye sud entertain sae strange a doubt!
My nephew and a Laird he canna be,
Were he a Laird, he'd be nae kin to me.

SANG IV

Knight   Tune—*Logen Water*

Tho' Beggar's garb and doublet mean,
The Centre will still be seen,
Yet Poverty clothes are void of art,
To hide a mean and sordid heart.

Discerning eyes will soon perceive,
The man of Honour from the Knave,
However much disguis'd they seem,
They still emit some native beam

What he has been, and may remain your friend,
I do na doubt, but that kin to you he's near.
Tho' for your nephew he has pass'd wi' a',
From me, no garb can hide young SETON-HA

Bra O come, come only, i' the secret part!
God bliss your Honour, keep it like your heart.
For tho' he, else, has had her kind consent,
He disna want that Bess hersell sud ken't.

Kn. The cause I guess, he means, no doubt to prove,
Ere that be kent, the depth of Bessy's love.

And

And troth I think it wad be far frae kin',
For me to baffle him in this defign
I mean to act a far mair friendly part,
This night he's ken gin fhe be woith his heart.
But, I bedeen, maun fee young SETON-HA',
And ha'e fome private crack between us twa.
I'll ablins, gi'e him news he difna ken,
And help the mattei fooner to an end.

Bra 'Twill be in vain, fr, g n ye mean to try,
To turn his love frae her anither way.
He's o'er fau biowdent on the lafs, I'm feai,
For ony th ng but hei to work a cure.
Befide, he's pafs'd his woid and winna flinch,
For he's a man of Honour, ilka inch.

Kn. I ken he is, but he's oblig'd to you.

Bra The ne'er ae bit, it's neathing but what's true.
The neareft o' his kin, I'll lay my life,
Will nae prevent his making Befs his wife.

Kn Whate'ei my aim, let that ne'er fafh your head,
But, be affui'd, it will be for his guid ·
A , n ye wifh to fho v yourfell his fiiend,
Ye'll fee to fend him o'er the way bedeen.
And ye may tell him that he's kent to me.

Bra. I fal obey, whate'er your purpofe be.

[*Exeunt.*

ACT

ACT III. SCENE I.

PROLOGUE TO THE SCENE.

To please the ee and charm the ear,
Ilk rural sweet salutes you here,
The yellow whins, in bloom, appear,
          Out-thro' the birken shade ,
And by the water bubbling near,
          A pleasing din is made.
Hark ! to the rus'ling of the trees,
Fann'd by the gentle wyst rn breeze ,
And Kattie singing, at her ease,
          Wi' mickle mirth and glee,
Gin neither lass nor music please,
          In troth, it's ill to die.

SANG V.

Tune —*O bonny lass will ye ly in a Barrack*

MY Simon's come back , and my cares are all over,
He swears, by his Kate, he'll nae mair be a rover,
But strive what he can, still to add to her pleasure,
What lass, but would think such a lad is a treasure !

Tho' late, in his absence, I pin'd and lamented,
Now he's safe return'd, my heart is contented,
The pleasure I have in this day s happy meeting,
Repays me for a' my past sobbing and greeting

Anes mair, now delighted, I view the green fields,
And taste a' the sweets which kind Nature still yields ;
Nae langer sic beauties are irksome to me,
Altho' they remind me, dear Simon, of thee.

                                        Flow

Flow on then sweet river, your murmurs now please me,
Nae langer, in vain, will ye strive now to ease me,
Tho' late, on your banks, I sat sighing and mourning,
Nae mair, now, I sigh for my Simon's returning

Now, Bessy comes to take the air,
Wi' rosy cheeks and flowing hair,
And sna'-white bosom half ns bare,
Delightfu' sigh!
Whas'er has e'n, now lat him stare,
Wi' a' his might.

B E S S.

BLYTH may ye sing, I trow your heart is glad,
That ye, anes mair, ha'e gotten hame your lad.

Ka. To sing or dance, I'm now in proper tift,
My bairn, O Bess, has got an unco' lift!

Bess. This day, indeed, has been a day of thrift

Ka I'm just as merry as I ha'e to be.

Bess. Mony sic days may Kate and Simon see!
Lang may she bruik him, lang may her joys last,
And drown ilk painfu' thought ot a' that's past!

Ka. I thank you, Cousin, sae sall Simon too,
Anes he has kent how guid ye've been to me.
Ye was ay kinder to me than the lave,
I'll ne'er forget, wi' what concern, ye strave
To chear my heart, and keep my spirits up,
When I was mailtly like to tyn a' hope.
As lang's I live, next Simon's sell alane,
I'll look upon you as my kindest frien!

F   Sae

Sae great your kindness, when he was awa,
I sure I ne'er can pay the ha f.——

    Bess ————————————Fy, na!   [*Jeeringly.*

Since he's return'd, lat that ne'er fash your head,
He'll me pay that, g ' a' your debts be paid
I o' r ty to u Coufi haw'd,
Wi n he, poor la s, was like to turn her lad;
And she may pay me now gin she incline,
Since, in a ke' , I my Jo maun tyn.

    Ha. Ye'll tyn your Jo! na, Bessy, dinna jeer.

    Bess. It's gnapin' ea re ft, lafs, I mak' you fear.
Are la has woo'd me l g, and promis'd fair,
Forgets his promifes, and oos nae mair;
Nor d he hae me now and gi'e him gowd.

    Ha. O fe a lad ye d be all befto v'd
S n fo the loß I hope may fair,
He   e, I d at ye ca arn'y fpare.
Sc em ne fcu I rad, H Clordy Will,
Or n d l   e   e ay t ne H ll
T , et I g na b l's g te fool

    B. Ve fe ß on ken t   Sin e I ve guefs'd fae
I'll g   er, nes j   e neard ne tale,   [well.
And e full get t a ro , ti n a d hale
Ge   les wo me, ro , u ro , day.
    for f   , h e p t e fe   ph ,
   h ge   o ,
    pr   'd, t e   l be t ue,
P , I ß ny d g s o ne

                                                    I

I ha'e obferv'd, within this little wee,
He'd meet auld *Boby*, ere he met w.' me
Afore he us'd to bare his hediy pow,
Where'er we met and mak' an awkward bow,
But, now, whene'er I chance to come in fight,
He fcours awa, as he had ta'en a fright

   Ka And can ye guefs the caufe o' fic a change?
Whate'er it be, I m fure it's fomething ftrange

   Befs I believe I may. Ned is the man I doubt,
Wha lang has wanted to ding Geordy out
I eith cud fee, it ga'e him micle pain,
To think that Geordy had won far er ben;
And I am certain, as ye'll fhortly fee,
That he has caften ill, twift him and me,
In hopes, to him, I m yni be fe ing;
When anes I find that Geordy's turn d fe dry

   Ka He! ftupit beaft, I cud n think him fit
For fic a trick, he wants baith fenfe and wit

   Befs But ye're miften, ye dinna ken him be f,
The ftill-fow after eats up a' the drum
Fools are as cunning whiles as wifer fouk,
And I'm miften, gin Ned be ony gowk
I ha'e guid reafon too, for thinking fae,
What think ye Aunty her tle ither day?

   Ka I cudna fay, but I'll be fur to hear,
Gin it be ought that makes the matter clear.

   Befs As fhe was flowly creeping in the way,
Wi' birn o' girfe for fupper to the ky.

Juft

Juſt as ſhe turns the corner o' the park,
She hears ane ſinging, there, as blyth's a lark.
Sae down ſhe leans her burn upon a hirſt,
To hear the ſang, tak' ſnuff and get a reſt.
Liſtening ſhe ſtood, but didna liſten lang,
'Till ſhe fnds I'm the burden o' the ſang
Now Aunty's curious, nae doubt, to ſee
Wha 'twas, that ſang ſae merrily 'bout me.
To Edward's voice, ſhe thought it unco' like,
And ſhe wad tak' a peep in o'er the dyke.
Juſt as ſhe looks, the muſic ſtopping ſhort,
Ned gi'e a gauf, and cries o' nappy ſport!
Now that I've gotten Geordy's birſe ſet up,
I'm thinking Beſs's pride will dree a fup.
Or lang ſhe winna be ſae red to lack,
My project, now, I think bids fair to tak'
A' they unſeen, ſhe c'd diſtinctly hear,
But gi'es to lift, cauſe he was coming near.
Ey t a' ane, Ned comes forward to the ſlap,
But ſeeing Aunty, back a piece he lap,
And teets to ſee gin ſhe was looking there,
Syn jumps athwart the road, as ſwift's a hare,
I to the park, that lies juſt o'er anent,
Syn ſets again wi' bonnet ſet aslant,
And ſinging wi' the thought ſhe naething ſaw,
Rublit his hands, and ga'e his lugs a claw;
Syn made a hoſt, and glowr'd an ther way,
But looks about, as Aunty's coming by.

Ay

Ay Ned, says she, this is a liesome night!

It is, says he, I fear that birn's nae light.

Ye better lat me eafe ye o't a wee,

It winna be fae great a lift to me.

She ga'e him thanks, but faid it wad be wrang

To trouble him, she hadna far to gang.

It's in my gate, I'm juft come thro' the park,

Ga en to the Smith, fays he, about fome wark.

The fafh to me will be but fma' I'm fear—

Aunty trudg'd on as gin she didna hear.

When mutt'ring to himfelf, a cunning thief,

She heard him fay I'm glad that Lucky's deaf.

A this she taul' me, foon as she came hame,

And we, atwifh us, ha'e contriv'd a fcheme,

That will, ere night, gie's a' fome handfome game }

   Ka I fud be blyth that baith the lads were wrought,

And gin I can be ufefu', now, in ought,

I'll do my beft, gin it nae fecret be—

   Befs I ne'er had ane I wad keep up frae thee.

I wad ha'e taul' you a' the fport before,

But then I cudna enter on the fcore ;

As lang's ye was fae fair down in the mou',

It wadna dane to fpeak o' lads to you.

But now, I hope, ye're fit to join the fport

   Ka. Well lat me hear't, for troth I'm langing for't.

   Befs. My Aunty fteppit o'er the way, laft night,

And taul' juft a' the ftory to the Knight.

                                    As

As he had do't, his Honor likes the jo?,
And ne's ..baith as he had boun a.. ft
We ..ent and had, 'e is on the p..,
A.. d..s o'er by, to q..st..n George the d..y
H.. ll be here I trow, a..e enou..,
I.. ..ing 'o..r fnce he g.. d o.. th..Know.
A..a ve.. 'l..on..... ..re.. i..re..b...ight,
Mean time, I'll gang, I te r..it rac..'l th..ght,
In fearc.. o' Ned, the .. I.. fee I.. '..ne,
To gie m a teaze, and f.. .. I.. ..I L.. ..g
But what .. .. ..e?————

_Ki_ ————————————The f..r..e I t..nk 's gu..d,
And I f..'ll tell you, how I w..u proceed
Upon your part, I th..nk it will e w..fe,
C..n ve lay onv fir..fs on my advice
G..a..le f..d f..eak o love, as like he w..ll,
T..k' t..rt, o'er foon, the fport ye ..nna fpll
D..na at firf, as ufual, cauld ard fh..,
..ut feem as gin ha'f w..l..ng to comply,
..nd a' his motions 'tentively beha'd.

_B.fs._ Fearra but I f..ll tightl.. cook my lad.
T..e day, I hear, he is to be at wark,
Juft near Sir Archbald's, in the mickle park.
I'll gang and fee gin I can find him out.

_Ka._ But fhort finfyne, I faw h..m tak' that rout.
Whiftling he gaed, and looking unco' bl..th,
And, in his hand, he danc'd a bran-new fcyt..e,

As

As he gaed pechin out thro' the trees,
And ———————— H—— in a bleeze.
Gazing, I maist was blinded wi' the sight,
The sun was beating on the blade sae bright.

B fs. Weel I abe ga'en, but ere I gang awa,
To you I fain wad fae a word or twa
This short advice I reh to gie to you,
For Branky's nephew, now, nae langer woo

Ka How that ad ce, gin ye now, like to say?
Is't 'cause the lad himsell has won the day?

Bess. This far ye hear, lat that be as it may.
He needs nae help frae you his tale to tell,
I find the lad can court right well himsell.

Ka Ye may speak plainer, lass, gin ye incline,
As, by your mumping, I maist guess your mind.
Ere-while I kent he had the better part,
And now, I fee, he's gotten a' your heart.
Ae thing I ken, altho' I say't mysell,
Gin it be fae, ye needna shame to tell.
There's gentler fouks, wha hanna ha f his menfe,
Beside, he bears the bell for wit and fenfe.
Get him wha likes, she winna get an afs,
Whae'er she be, hell be a lucky lafs.
And ye'll be her, or else I'm fair mista'en,
Ye ha'e his heart——

B fs. ————————And he has mine I ken.

Ka Well heart for heart, my Beffy, is but fair,
The bargain's only equal and nae mair.

Gin

Gin it be fae, and ye fud ken youfell,
It's only fair, I think, that ye fud tell
Tell him ye love, and dinna live in pine,
But eafe, at anes, your ain and Jamie's mind.
Nor fear to do't, ye ll ne'er ha'e caufe to rue,
I'fe lay my life, ye'll find him kind and true.

Befs I wifh he prove nae war than what ye fay,
For, to be plain, I taul him a' the day.
Cafe he, like ither lads, meant to beguile,
To gar him think me cauld I ftrave a while,
But ilka word he fpake was weal d fae fweet,
It wafna lang into my pow'r to do't.
He woo'd fae warm, I was oblig'd to yield,
And own him fairly Mafter o' the Field.

SANG VI.

Tune.—*My Lodging is on the cold ground.*

I Met my dear Jamie returning to day,
  And with him retir'd to yon grove
Where, with pleafure, I heard what th' youth had to fay,
For all his difcourfe was o' love

  So warmly he prefs d, that ere I was aware,
He flily had ftowen a kifs,
Yet, I fan my heart cou'd not blame him fo far,
As allow me to take it amifs

  His love, with fuch fweetnefs endearing, he told,
I heard his kind tale with content,
And thought it but vain to appear longer cold,
When I found my heart beating confent

In his arms I fell, and with look of regard,
For I could be no longer unkind;
To Jamie my feelings I freely declar'd,
And honestly open'd my mind.

With rapture he heard the confession I made,
And swore he would love me thro' life,
And, with the sweet hope, my Jamie here now is glad,
That to Jamie I'll soon be a wife.   [Exeunt.

SCENE II.

PROLOGUE TO THE SCENE

A bra' grass park, set round wi' trees,
Where are ray lo'll, a while, at ease,
And t see the fragrance o' the leaves,
          N   a ages near
While bum of busy   ,
          D

See, back, a tune   sit e the sheep,
In stands, rejoicing to map,
      ,   , en usp the
Hear would be   , ye   he's up o

I hae some hopes my scheme will now succeed,
It's been lang about'tnoth it may be guid
To win her love has cost me meikle pain,
But now I think, proud Bess, I hae my ain.
How far 'twas right to blot out Bess's fame,
I winna say, but sure, it was nae game;
And tho', in that, I pay'd a   part,
What say, by that, but I may gain her heart.
          G.   For

For what altho' she didna prove half kind,
Whan I endeavour'd, first, to tell my mind.
She then, wi' Geordy, held an unco' fyke,
But, there, the butter's casten to the tyke,
And I may chance to ha'e some better hap,
I'll do my speed to catch her in the trap.
For, now, I'd think she wad ha'e better will,
To hear o' love, gin I ha'e ony skill.
For lasses, when their wooers chance to change,
Aft stretch a point, to get a just revenge.
Be as it may, I am resolved to try,
How matters wag, I see her come this way.

He sings, and Bess behin' a tree,
Stands, for a while, to hear and see

S A N G.   VII

Tune —Woo'd, and married, and a'.

I lo'e bonny Bess,
   But ch, alas! wae's me!
I lo'e bonny Bess,
But Bess likesna me!

   First, when I taul' my mind,
She leugh at a' my care,
But, now, her Jo's unkind,
And laughs at her as fair

   To slight sae sweet a prize,
O what an ass is he!
I wad be far mair wise,
Cud she but think o' me.

Were

Were she o' me as fun,
I'd nae be cauld nor sh,,
He ne'er cud sha v disdain,
Gin he had lov'd as I

BESS entering the Park

Bess Ned ha'd ye busy, ay in merry mood,
Singing, they say, whiles gars the wark come speed
Gin that be true, in sic a bonny day,
Ye'll mak' an unco' hole amang the hay
Sing on, and dinna lat me pit you wrang,
I didna mean to stop you in your sang

Ned. Sindle I sing, by what I us'd to doe,
And wark I fear will get sma' sh with frae me
I hinna been myfell, this mony lang,
Nowther at wark nor singing of a sang.
Wha has a heart sae borne down in' wae
Will but ill far'dly owther sing or say.
When a' was right, I then cud blythly sing,
And wi' my music gar the woodlands ring
Baith even and morn, I was ay blyth and gay,
And whistled a' my little cares away
But times, my bonny Bess, are alter'd sair,
And merry thoughts are buried, now, in care'

Bess What ails thee Ned? gin life o'er hard to sper,
Gin ye have health, ne'er grumble cause ye're poor.
Fouks wha ha'e little, can lat little tyn,
Ne'er lat the Warld brak' your peace o' mind.

In

In ye ken, there's mony an up and down,

A ... of fortune ... may br... your crown;

She'll ... ... and to ... and heal the wound,

C... a presence, c...ly bear the ftound

W... and from, a dye ma... ft'rd relief,

A men... heart and ... be fla... to grief

... has enough, my Bess, can ne'er be poor,

I... ... for the want o' gear

I... ... makes a ... a rs m... ul,

... ... th... a mierter fouks can tell.

C... ... ..., the ... fome h...e lefs th... me,

That I ... high ... e... ge... fortune wi',

T... I's, I'm ... content, is ... to bear,

T... ... ... of fulk's gear.

S... ... ... fuln my ... ,

T... I'... ... Im fo ... fet in a law

Were ... ... I ... ... mak' a fhift,

C... ... fallen to g... ... ... by thrift.

But... ... ...h that I a... ke to d...e,

I... ... ... o' n...!

... ... to happen, ne er fafh your thum',

I s... ... ng to ... ... that are to come.

L... ... ..., and o... th cark and care,

I... ... ..., ... d... ... defpair.

A' ... a pa... ... ... hangs,

I... ... ... from fed-to ... e's fangs.

E... ... we ... the greateft danger near,

S... lucky turn a... cheats us of our fear.

Whale's

Whare's Coufin Kattie, there, ayon' the burn,
Her fears, I trow, ha'e ta en a happy turn
Tho' for this ouk, her heart has been right grite,
And few but thought that fhe wad get the bite.
Yet Simon's come, whafe ab'ence ga'e her pain,
And fhe well pleas'd, fees t' her fears were vain.
Keep up your heart, Ned, never let it fa',
Anes tyn the heart, and bid farewell to a'.

Ned A' leff r cares, my Beffy, I d fhun,
It s far frae eafy, that makes me complain.
Kate has been lucky, fae has Simon too,
And ilk ane happy in his love but me !
Were I as happy in my love is they,
I'd find nae room into my heart for wae
But wha cud bear to find his bofom burn,
Wi' honeft love, and yet meet nae return !
The cafe is hard, and yet that cafe is mine,
I like a lafs, and yet fhe is unkind !
Keep up my heart, it's na't fo eafy dane,
She'll be my dead, that will be fhortly feen !

Befs Wow ! Ned, ye h nna ha'f enough o' pride,
Or ye mith well fae fma' a benfil bide !
De for a lafs ! I thought ye far man wife,
Gin fhe be faucy, ye fud e'en be nice.
Were I a lad, it ne'er fud gi'e me pain,
Tho I fud get the na-fay man, frae ten.
The laffes arena, now o' days, fo fcant,
Tho' ane be proud, ye needna fear ye'll want.

Ye

Ye may get twenty full as fair as she,
And full as guid, however guid she be.

Ned Nane haf so guid I ken, nor ha'f so fair,
Tae er fan ane, wi' her that wad compare!
Tho' ane, my Bess, she sa' to me,
And, but hersel, nae ither lass will doe!
I ne'er cud bear in a' m life, to range,
The lo e's rae deep, that can sae easy change
Sightner' na, na I hinna tin my pow'r,
And gin I lo her, I will ne er cowr!
Bess, may f git, but then were Bess like me,
She wad fee matters wi' a ither ee!

Bess Poor that ony, lass sud lightlie you,
Few lads are, now o' days, in love sae true.
It's hard that she sud slight, and ye so fain,
Pity, nae ither lass can ease your pain.
What can she be, that's lo d by sic a youth,
And wad aout to quench his lovin' drouth!
She ill deserves to get sae gud a lad,
That she dinna rue and tyn her la'd

Ned Gin Bess pities, lat her pity shaw,
It's in her pow'r to put an end to a'
But her, nae lass cu'd ever gar me smart,
But her, nae ither can lift up my heart!

SANG.

SANG VIII

Tune.—*A' the Whigs will gae to Hell*

A' The night, I figh and mourn,
    Bonny laffie, lowland laffe,
Nor find my reft, with day, return,
My bonny lowland laffie

It brings frefh marks of your difdain,
Bonny laffie, &c
    Which fair but to increafe my pain,
My bonny lowland laffe

Whene'er I fpeak of love, ye frown,
Bonny laffie, &c.
    And that pits a' my courage down,
My bonny lowland laffie

Gin ye ae kindly look wad wear,
Bonny laffie, &c
    A' this gloom wad difappear,
My bonny lowland laffie

But, gin ye dinna deign to fmile,
Bonny laffie, &c
    There's nought, in life, that's worth my while,
My bonny lowland laffie!

In Death's embrace, then only laid,
Bonny laffie, &c
    I may reft and peace maun find,
My bonny lowland laffie!

Befs.

Bess Ay, Ned, that's news ye tell me, man, indeed,
I thought that Bess had worn out o' head
She's left by ane wha woo'd man baul' than you,
And promis'd just as fairly to be true.
This mony day, ye never ment on'd love.

   Ned Because I saw my Bess wad ne'er approve,
What need I woo, when that but eeks my pain,
Since kind expressions only meet disdain
Had I been, ever, likely to come speed,
Love, and love only, had been a my leed.
But dinna jeer me, Bess, lat me be,
Ye never wad, nor e'er will pity me!
Some happier lad nor me is far'er ben,
This lang I thought, and now the truth I ken.
But tho' we get him, he'll be dearly bought,
He'll ne'er shaw you the kindness that he ought.

   Bess Wha is't that Ned can think I like sae well?

   Ned Are wha cud pass you, Bess, to the Deil!
Wha wad gie gowd, but that he's scant o' gear,
That he o' Bess and a' her charms was dear
And ser, we are ae gude a prize sed sin,
Ard, wi' his Honor said, wad keep the gap.
Forgie me, bonny Bess, gin I'm o'er plain,
I fain wad save you frae a life o' pain.
What, tho' his Honor my gai George agree,
Ye ne'er will be sae happy as wi' me
Ye ne'er need hope a single happy day,
Forc'd pray'rs are nae devotion, as they say.

'Twere

'Twere right, I think, ye tak' your ain advice,
As he is faucy, ye fud e'en le

Gi'e love for love, and him, was I ates difpife,
It's in your pow'r, my Befs, to turn the guife.

Befs I'll need a thought, ere ony thing I fay,
But I maun leave you, Simon comes this way
I wadna like to lat a lover die,

Ned aline

I'm glad to hear't, but troth it's nae be me.
Die for a lafs ! na faith I'm nae fo foo',
The laffes, firft, may a' gae to the De'il
With me, love ifna yet fo freely deep,
Nor ever fall, or it's be thro' my fleep !
For a' her beauty, I the laft cull of,
Lat me but get my clooks on aunty's poze.

Enter Simo

I'll warrant ye've been courting Befs e'en now,
O Ned there's little wit, man, in your pow.
Gin ye maun die for her, e'en ftop your fyke,
And mak' your teft'ment, Ned, where er you lie.
Think ye, fhe'll ever look the gate o' you ?

Ned. I've feen as great a fairey, tho' fhe do
Simon mith had his tongue, gin he were wife,
His ain lafs ftamach difna fee n o er nice !
Nane cud caft up, tho' I were Befs's lad,
I ever wore the bonnet and cockade !

Kn. What, dare ye fay, ye bladderheaded afs,
Either to me, or yet about my lafs ?

H   Gi s

[*Gives Ned a cuff and drives off his bonnet.*

Ned Simon, nae doubt, is to the fighting bred,
But I can pay this debt, tho' nae my trade.

[*Returns the cuff, and Simon turns up his heels.*

GEORGE *entering suddenly, gives Simon a cuff as he
speaks.*

Geo Stop gin ye're wife, what can this brullie
I fain wad ken your busness wi' my frien'' [mean !

Sim I dinna fear twa fools, tho' I'm alane.
Of what he gets, ye're welcome to a share,

[*Strikes George.*

I dinna think I'll yield to se a pair !
Come on my lads,

[*A battle and Simon beats them both off.*

Simon and Ned —————— But dinna rug our hair !

K Ye cowardly tykes, I scorn sic silly game !

George and Ned O ! mercy ! mercy !

Ned ———————————Simon, I'm to blame !

ACT

ACT IV. SCENE I

PROLOGUE TO THE SCENE.

A flow'ry walk extended wide,
With lofty elms on ilka side
Whase meeting taps h de a' aboon,
But gin ye, laigher, look between;
Ye, first, observe the clear blue sky,
Then, laigher still, ye charm the eye,
With woods, and groves, and flow'ry fields,
And a' the sweets which Nature yields
Anes take your fairin' of the sight,
Syn, when ye think ye've view'd a right,
Your eyes, to nearer objects, move,
And tent a youth that's blist in love.

Jamie alane.

SANG IX

Tune—The yellow-hair'd Laddie

HOW happy the youth, when to love he's inclin'd,
Who finds his dear fair, like my Bessy, prove kind,
So extreme is his joy, his pleasure so great,
Tho' I feel, I can't tell you, how happy his state!

All description it baffles, no words can impart
One half of the blifs, which he feels in his heart;
Her consent obtain'd, such emotions arise,
He would burst, if they found not a vent at his eyes!

Enter BRANKY.

Ja. Well, have ye founded Helen on the match?
I think ye hanna made o'er quick difpatch.

I doubt fhe hafna been fae eafy pleaf'd,
As what ye thought —

Dia —————————Troth, fir, ye are refus'd
Ara gin ye dinna, like yourfell, appear,
Ye'll nee get Befs, wi' her confent, I fear.
Ye mun fhak' aff that becoming drefs,
Or elfe gie o'er a' thoughts o' getting Befs.

Ja I think roor nephew mair than fhe fud flight,
But maybe, Befsy naena roos'd him right.
Ye fud ra'e toul' his virtues ane by ane,
And fyn begun again, when ye had dane.
And gin ye fan that a' that ye adna doe,
Ne'er fcrupl'd, man, to gie him twa or three

Bia. Gin I fa'd nought but guid, I cudna be
I cnly tau' the truth and naething mair,
Altho' I roos'd you to her, lang and fair
Sne far, fhe heard your virtues werena few,
A better lad, fays I, ne'er trade the dew
A fairer lad, nor are o' greater thrift,
I'm fair ye're o ckh'd hap, er to the lifr
Tho' fe are y f ud, I tu ra ory fhame,
He fays es hur fo turhan I can name,
And bad ye let ina ha'b your niece a wife,
An fure fce here a very happy life.
To' here's g e, I lhen e fa poor,
He ca a sut enoig o' gcods and gear
fhe'll ha e as lith a biede es can be found,
In a ue ccu tr e fee t round and round

Ja. Troth, friend, I think ye've roos'd right well
I wonder that ye camena better speed   [indeed,

  Bra. And sae ye may, fae ony ane mith think,
But I'se assure ye, Helen's nae sma' drink !
It's nae to ilka chiel she'll gi'e her niece,
There's few wad think her sie a saucy piece !

  Ja. What reason gives she for her disregard ?

  Bra. Nae ither, sir, but that ye're nae a Laird
And were ye not, I fear ye'd be ahin,
I never in my life, sir, heard sic win' !
I b'leve she thinks Bess match for ony he,
That ever steppit in a leather shoe
Her like, for beauty, says she, I cou'd lay,
Ye scarce wad see, in a lang simmer's day.
Nor does a better draw the breath o' life,
A Laird, wi' joy, mith simle on sic a wife
And I may live to see as gude a sport,
As sma' a ship has won as gude a port
On hearing this, I bade her a guid day,
'Twas beating o' the air, to wis I to stay !
I'll say nae mair, e'en now, I wad awa,
And lat you think, says I, your pride may fa'.
I kenna, says she, sic a thing mith be,
But then, I hope, it's what ye winna see
It's nae thro' slight, I wad your frien' deny,
Nor yet, without a cause, I look sae high
And what's sae mighty cause, sir do ye think ?

Ja. Maybe auld Lucky likes a drap o' drink.
Gin that's the cafe, I think it nae ways ftrange,
On fome the timmer works an unco' change.
It mony times has dane as mighty things,
Beggars, when drunk, have fancied themfelves Kings,
Marhap it's turn'd auld Helen to a Queen,
And Befs into a Princefs of the Green.
Nae wonder, then, fhe think a Laird mith fmile,
A Princefs wad be fomething worth his while.

Bra Troth, fir, I wad been ready to fuppofe,
That fome chiel had fet up auld Helen s nofe;
But that I ken fhe is a fober wife,
And ne'er was kent for ither a her life
That's nae the caufe, ye'll need to guefs again,
Or tak' hale twenty o' them, a' on end;
And after a', I doubt gin ye wad light,
Amang a harder mair, upon the right.
It s fomething ftrange, ye'll ferly, fir, to hear't,
She taul' me a', ere I gat time to fpeir t.
Sometime ago, fhe had Befs fortune read,
By ane, it feems, a deacon at the trade.
Wha taul' fic things, I'm fure nae ane cud tell,
Unlefs fome *Warlock* or auld *Nick* himfell.
But Helen tells me that fhe now ther faw,
Gin he was horn'd or had a cloven pa't

Ja It s been the humble Devil, then that's a'.
Bra. Fuith, like enough He had a laug black beard!
Ja And, how, did Helen fay he difappeai'd?

                                        Bra.

Bar. He ſtay d nae langer than he taul' his tale,
Nor wad he tak' her ſiller or her meal.
Right aſt he gae'd, and in amang the trees,
She cudna tell me gin ſhe ſaw them bleeze!
But ſays ſhe never ſaw him mair finſyne.

Ja. He's been a Devil of a generous kind,
To gie ſo great a fortune to her Niece,
And neither tak her ſiller nor a piece.
But yet, perhaps, he may again appear,
And crave the laſs, when anes ſhe gets the gear
He'll ha'e a chance to be ſome better ſair'd,
By Beſs herſell, when anes ſhe gets the Laird.

Bra I doubtna but ſhe ll think his title guid,
When a' comes true he did ſae wiſely read.
But faith, I fear, forgie me gin I tell,
That ye have been this gen'rous De'il yourſell

Ja I ſee, my friend, that ye right well can gueſs,
And that I hinna play'd my part amiſs
I'm g'ad my ſcheme is like to take ſae well,
And that auld Lucky liſten'd to the tale

Bra. Like Goſpel, ſir, ſhe credits a' ye ſaid,
And ſays, ſhe's ſure, 'twill happen as ye read.
For part, this day, ſhe ſays, has come to paſs,
O' what ye archly ſpaed about the laſs.

Ja. Ye ſee, then, Branky, ane may ſpae right well,
Wha iſna juſt in compact wi' the De'il
And tho' nae born wi' the ſecond ſight,
He may, if wyly, ſpae a fortune right.

Bra.

Bes. I do na hear yo , wha cud better ken,
How things were gaen' or gueis how they wad end ?

Ja. And fac it is with a the fpaeing crew
Gin they e traight on on trug that's true,
Tho , fot, r oun learnt, by fome trick of art,
Leare they e rer on the pueing part.
Th re ghtous, af , t   ea what truth they tell,
and w ues, by cun ng, than wuk folks themfell .
Marn g , touo, what a e s tru may hear,
To w t que os, me ther ar ly fpeir.
Man ue new ure tren, ti , in the face,
To fee at approune one can t ace
And gr ten, t is, b , ot they hear and fee,
They en w en they na ver anc on a le.
For ans th , fid they have ae truth expreft,
Th re fure to get a creut for the reft
ca , t en, at Fortune's happy turns may guefs,
Ic ues hae that, a e never ta'en a fs
'Tis in t e o the crud fouer apofe,
And thue they get em wor cro they, difclofe
Tenretu's ignorance t f u they craw,
Wule, to the Day, ful i gate it o'

Bes. In frith, I t on you now, wi' a' my heart,
Ye feem to ken the huus, fir o' t e art
P ain cult y fonus are eafily outfeen,
But Book-lear'd men, like you, ha'e cla er een.
Yet, for m fel', I never, a' my days,
Has m al e fa h a fore men, o their fays.

Nei

Nor did I, ever, wi' a single plack;
E'er cross the lure of ony o' th' pack.
Tho' aften blam'd by sic fool sort o' folks,
Wha li'd to cast their siller at the cocks;
Because, wi' mair reverence I beta'd,
But leugh to see them ——lin,'t, deceiv'd,
When, roun'd the ta'le, in a bonnach set,
I've seen a dizen fdgin for their sate,
And ilk ane's fortune turning up a grate,
As he was hor'd in the render's race
Fortune ay favouring that fool the maist,
Wha coft'd her favours, at the greatest cost.
While a' were, wi' their luck, right well content,
Nor thought it ill bestow'd what they had spent,
As Lasses wad be L——ers o' *fighen*',
And Plough-men, in a short, set up a B——'
But yet the day I mourn, in confidence, o' n,
I wi' some doubtis' o' the matter grew
When ——den trad' sae mony, tauga' true,
That the eud get, but some lar, or you

To Freem, she gat the bale, and my design
Is l——n, now, to advise to my mind
At L——s treatment I'm made very displeas'd,
I had her ——ding, had we been kinder us'd.
For, I, this sennes, I hope, curling, to prove,
The lass of best ——— my love.
Her Aunt a —''d, soon, in —— ac ear,
And how she takes the news, I'll quickly hear.

I

Bra. I thought that ye had only fpae'd for fport,
But now, I find ye've wifer reafons for t.
Yet, what gin, after a' that ye have dane,
Ye be difcover'd by fome grite rich friend,
Whafe pride wad never bear that ye fud wed,
A Cottage Beauty and a hame-fpun maid?
Counfell'd by fic a ane, ye yet mith rue,
And bid fair Befs and a' her charms adieu.
For cuftom, now o' days, wad feem to prove,
Fouks ought to marry mair for gain than love.
And ane that's poor is lack'd tho' ne'er fo guid,
As poor and rich were no ae flefh and blood

Ja Whatever notions high-born fools may frame,
The mould of poor and rich is juft the fame,
No finer blood rins in a Princefs' veins,
Than paints the cheek of Befsy of the Plains.
Nor would I give this Beauty of the Green,
With all her fweetnefs, modeft look, and mien,
To be connected with the richeft Queen !

S A N G   X

Tune—The Miller of Dee

THE lad, who gaes courting for greed of the cafh,
   Looking lefs at the lafs than the gold,
If he barters his peace for a bundle of trafh,
And though that he fhould

Pl re er gae a wooing for fake of the gear,
It were baff to pleafe in herfelf,
I never ll fight her, becaufe fhe is poor
and has no a pen worth

Nor

Nor will I e'er think it below me to wed,
When a lass of true merit I find
Nor care I farthing how humble the maid,
If she is but loving and kind

Tho' proud-hearted Coxcombs may say it is merit,
To marry beneath my degree
I care not, by such, how my conduct is seen,
It is of no moment to me

In choosing a darling companion for life,
For myself, I'm determin'd to judge,
And if I am pleas'd to make Bessy my wife,
Who else has a title to grudge?

Bra Well ha'd ye sae, for I was eich to tell
A circumstance, which, 'mang the rest, befell,
As I was gaen frae Helen's, by the way,
I saw the Knight, and wish'd him a guid day,
For you he speir'd; I thought he naething knew,
And taul' him a' 'bout Helen, Bess, and you
I ga'e the tale a sort o' hidden cast,
Thinking ye, for my Nephew, wi' him past.
But, in a short, to my nae sma' surprise,
I fan he kent the Laird, thro' the disguise!
How ye may like it, sir, I dinna ken

Ja The news, my friend, give me no kind of pain.
By him my Bessy has been kindly us'd,
And, at her luck, he canna be displeas'd.
This day, she taul' me, when we were alane,
In him, she, lang, has had a worthy friend.

A

A thousand ways, she said, he had been guid,
And ????? Bess, when she ??ch?d to read:
To whi??, ?? ?? be?? b????s of her mind,
W??? ?, ???? ?, ???? more e????ed, find.
Be???? ?? ????? ????? of our t??e,
C? ??? ?? ??gh? ???? ?? ?, and best.
T?? ????? ?? ?? ??? ??? to co??ell,
A?? ????? ??elds ot ????? ?? the foul.
I ???? ??? ??????? ?? once ?mp?rt,
A?? ?????? ???, ???? ther ?mp??ve the heart.
????? vacant ???? ?? t?de, ? ?????? ???t,
H?? f???, do ?? f?d the moments spent ?
T??? g???? ????? from reading flow,
???? ???? ????? ??'???? ?n know!

  B? V????, g? ?? be re d? to comply,
F?? ??? ????? ???? ?? ?? ad gang o?r by.
??? ???????? ???? ?? la?? to tell,
??? ?? ???????? ?? ?? yourf?l,
??? ?? ? to p?? ???? ? way t? know,
T??? ?? ???? be ???? ?? our love ?r ro.
  ?? ????? ???? ?? ??n, with a' my 'hear?,
A ???? ???? ??? ?? ??? may ?? p?rt.
I b?? ?? ?? ? ?? ????? worth,
??? ??? s on ???? ?areless of ?t's birth.
C?? ?? ??? ???? ?? one so nobly kind,
T?? ?? ??? ??, ???ch cherish'd, and refin'd, ⎫
??? ??? ?? ??, and ???ead, and bloming blifs mankind. ⎬
                                                     ⎭

[*Exeunt.*

SCENE.

SCENE II.

PROLOGUE TO THE SCENE

It's Helen's dwall'ng, view it weel,
For it can bide a look,
Auld Lucky sitting, at L r reel,
Ben, in the Pantry noo
Excuse, for she, a wee, maun fuck,
Just, as ye heard the reel, che k,
By some wrung cadge she o'e her hand,
She's tint her end, and maun stand
'Confess's but weak o' fish,
'Till raxing to the chimney-stan,
She, shortly, finds two fesfu' eer,
That help to mend her light,
Whilk anes applied o h r of,
To wark, thus comes, she go,
First, meets the pirn, and turns it round about,
'Till, wi' a pirn, she presses the tint end out,
      A dteely draws it loofe,
Syn, to the reel, anes, tightly tied,
Down, in the self, she lays it d
      Her een, for after if
And, now, by cautious turns and flow,
Anes mair, she gars the reel go

SANG XI

Tune — Twitly Tittie, or the Archer's March

THO' Boreas lang, may rudely bla',
  And hill and dale be clad wi' fna',
Yet, gloomy Winter wears awa,
    And joyfu' spring appears

        Then,

Then, Nature, anes mair, smiling,
Ilk silly tear beguiling,
With plenty, crowns the toiling
    Of busy Industry

Tho' lang he's bow'd 'neath Fortune's blast,
My Bessy will won up, at last,
My Bessy, now, wons up, at last,
    And happier days appear

Soon, shall I see her smiling,
A' my past fears beguiling,
The thought repays my toiling,
    For her, this mony day

This night, I'll tell a story,
Will make them blyth and sorry,
Will make them blyth and sorry,
    At the strange turns of Fate!

While hearing, they shall wonder,
And cat a wily blunder,
But, kent for truth, like thunder,
    Will fixe them wi' amaze

It, then, will be nae spring of wo!
'Cause he has wedded ane o'er low,
'Cause he has wedded ane o'er low,
    And far beneath his rank.

Her, soon, his equal he shall see,
And, wi' the ane, delighted he,
His heart and hand, content, shall gi'e,
    And blifs his happy fate

And, when, in wedlock they are join'd,
May they ilk comfort in it find,
May they ilk comfort in it find,
    Which e'er that state could yield

                      Love

Love, wi' their days, increasing,
Lang may they live, possessing,
Ilk joy, and earthly blissing,
    Kind Heav'n can bestow!

O Providence! now, hear me,
And, in the evening, cheer me,
And, in the evening, cheer me,
    Of my declining age!

Thy Goodness, then, admiring,
To greater joys aspiring,
I'll pleas'd, frae life, retiring,
    Ly down amang the Dead!

Missing a fit, upon the outer door,
Dory flytes in, and raises up a roar.

Dor   Whare are ye, oman?—Helen, are ye, here?
                           [*Coming ben.*

Hel   She's nae far aff, but what mak's a' the steer?
Dor   Preserve me! oman, are ye, yet, sae fool,
As think o' wark—gae and throw by the reel.
Leave that to fouks wha ha'e their bread to won,
Gin ye'd be grite, ye sudna reel nor spin;
By them, it's thought wark borders on a sin
They scarce can bear to ha'e it in their sight   [sight

Hel.   Gae wi' your stuff, I think your head's turn'd
Dor   When Bess grows Lady, ye may spare the
I'll warran this is for the bridal sark   [wark,
Fool wife, to think, when anes she gets a Laird,
She'll be set by wi' ought ye'll spin or kard!

                               The

The Laird she gets, will be but unco' poor,
Gin he's nae fit to gi'e her better gear.
In silks and sattins, he will gar her shine,
And gi'e her cuffs made o' the Holland fine.
Like i'ther Ladies, in her braws she'll sail,
And be new moulded sae, baith head and tail,
She'll nae be kent, by auld acquaintance, more,
Nor aiblins, ken them, as she did afore

BA. Na, Theodore, I hope nae change of state,
Will e'er make Bess her former friends forget.
She has mair sense, I hinna ony fear,
She'll e'er slight auld acquaintance, 'cause they're poor,
That's but the case, when fools to fortunes rise,
Less bliss'd wi' sense, than those whom they despise.
But are of sense, who rise to be great,
Will still regard those of less happy fate.

Gin I' that a' are, equally, the care,
Of fate and Providence, which plac'd them, there;
When some as are, and lots or they fi',
Let us learn, still to a' be to a'.
Who'd be proud of on happy lot,

. . . .

When some . . . .

Of wit and fenfe, fud yet fae fooli'h be,
As liften to a tale fie like a lie.
Befs get a Laird ! I laugh, troth, in my fleeve,
To think ye fud fae ftrange a tale believe.

Hel. Ye a' may laugh, fince laughing does nae ill,
She'll get the Laird, and ye may laugh your fill

Dor Well, gin fhe get him, lat it e'en be fae,
At Beffy's luck, I'm fure, I'll no be wae,
I'fe be as blyth as Helen, on that day.
Gin bra' rich Ladies meet wi fuch neglect,
And fhe fic luck, it's mair than I expect,
It wad be ftrange, fud fic gite things appear,
In days, when fouks rin wid on Warlds-gear.
The lafs is bonny, and, nae doubt, fhe's guid,
But nowther rich, nor come o' gentle blood

Hel. Be 'at fhe like, that s nowther here, nor there,
Sud Ladies want, a Laird will be her fhare
Ye're a' nif-wife, but ere ye fleep, this night,
Ye'll, maybe, fee wha's far'eft in the right
Fouks will turn Lairds, mayhap, ye thinkna o',
Wha, like my Beffy, look, e'en now, but low.
And as grite ferlies, adiins, fome h'e feen,
As fhe turn Lady, ere the night be dane.

Dor. Gin e'er fic wonders fall be brought to light,
Nane will be mair delighted wi' the fight
Seeing's believing, a' the Warld allow,
And great will be my joy your tale prove true

K   But

P. ... ... th . . Cow,
O... ... ..., ... then Jo?
... ... l nat'e o' them fkaith,
P... th ... ... t p'e fe them ba h.
The row ae reafo is gud, I fhft his claim,
V... c furd'. es to g... b, fie a name
Lie'ing ve'l ye fe., g. a ye in health be fpar'd,
This Bro ky's Nephew fhat into a Laird

Dw. For God's caufe, Helen, will ye a' explain,
Or ye'l gae near to turn me in the brain!
O dinna round about your ftory hint,
For, now, I doubt there's mair than nonfenfe in't!

He! I wadna care, but ye maun hool frae a',
Whate'er I tell ye now, atwifh us twa.

Dor. Ye needna fear, by me it's ne'er be taul',
What ye difclofe, I'll keep it like my faul

He. Then liften, and ye ilka thing fall hear,
As far as I can hippen to your ear.
Ae afternoon, a litle while finfyne,
I hope, wi' joy, I'll ay that day remind.
A heavy fhow'r came pouring frae a cloud,
Blue lightening flafh'd, and thunder rumbl'd loud, }
Wi' fearfu' din, amang the hills and wood.
When, frae the braes, a' wet and out o' breath,
A bra' young lad came running thro' the heath,
Wi' dog and gun, and as luck fair'd, was fain,
Within my Cruve, to fhelter frae the rain.

When

When he was set, I gi'e the fire a stir,
And Bess ran and brought some whins, wi' vir,
Frae o't the nook, and laid a lowin bleeze,
To dry his cl'es and gar him sit at ease
He said, he had been in the Hill i' dry,
And seem'd quite faint and weary wi' the play
Says I, to Bess, I think ye'll better try,
Gin he wad drink some milk new frae the ky.
Meanwhile, in haste, I laid upon the board,
Some cruds and ream, the best I cud afford
Says he, I blush ye sud sic trouble take,
I wis', says I, 'twere better for your sake
We ha'e but little fit for guests like you,
But sic's we ha'e, we mak' you welcome to
He thank'd us, very kindly, for our care,
And said a King might feast upon sic fare :
But, as he never lik'd to sup, alone,
He smil'd, and begg'd that Bess wad tak' a spoon.
She thank'd him for the complement he meant,
And, after some intreaty, blush'd consent.
Nor wad he taste, but loot his cutty lie,
Till she agreed, at least, to shaw the way,
Syn roof'd my cruds, and said, to eek my praise,
He ne'er had feasted better, a' his days.

Dor Gin ye was able to keep down your pride,
It's something strange, that speech was far to bide!
Hel. I'm glad, says I, ye think the feast so good,
But well kent I, what feast was understood

I

I thought it plain, frae what I'd heard and feen,
It m're juft the cruds that he cud mean.
It vad be vain to tell you a' he faid,
O half the compl'ments, to Befs, he paid
It lang was fair, afore he thought o' ga'en,
And gm't on to evening now was drawn
When up he rafe, to mak' a lang tale fhort,
And bade's gud night, but feem'd right forry for't.
Clapping her fhou'der as he left the door,
He f..d he ne'er fav Beffy s mak' before,
And that, gin e'er they chanc'd to meet again,
She rauh ha'e caufe to thank the fhow'r o' rain.
And now, ere lang, I hope it will be true,
In Branky's Nephew, I this youth can view.
As foon es, firft I faw him in this place,
For a' his ftrange difgufe, I kent the face.

Dor O how my heart s delighted wi' the tale!

Hel Ye'll like it better, as es ye kent the hale.
But ifna't ftrange that Beffy fudna fee,
Lauin rer lover, v hen s feen by me ?
But fhe poor lafs, vhen firft acquaint, was fhy,
Nor e'er, without a pufh, cud look his way.
As fure, where er fhe did, to meet his een,
When I n itl' looked half an hour, unfeen.

Dor But difna Beffy, yet, fome notion ha'e,
How things are ga'en, or how the're like to gae ?

Hel Nae e'en the leaft, as yet fhe difna know,
How I us'd Branky and refus'd her Jo.

Dor.

Dor. But, whare-to did ye't, oman, lat me hear?
To ken the Laird, and flight him, troth was quear.

Hel. I ha'e dane naething but by guid advice,
And what the Knight conhders fit and wife.
Wha was it, think ye, did fae flyly tell,
My Beffy's fortune, but the lad himfell?
Sane after, fhe gae'd hame to fair the Knight,
Ae evening, juft 'bout dwauming o' the light,
As I was fitting in the houfe, alane,
An auld-like Carle fteppit in, bedeen,
A hat fair floutch'd, and wi' a gartan tied
Aneath his chin, fair'd a' his face to hide,
Except his beard, which was baith fleek, and lang,
And like a gvat's, maift to his breaft, it hang.
About his fhou'ders was a duddy cloak,
And, in his hand, a knotted branch of oak.
Goodwife, he fays, I fain wad reft a while,
I'm wearied fair, tho' I've fcarce gane a mile.
I've feen the day, but my beft days ate o'er,
I wadna been fae wearied wi' a fcore!
Auld joints, fays he, are ftiffer than the green,
And need a reft, fays I, ye're welcome friend.
When he was fet, and after fome fhort crack,
He flyly looft me ken he had a knack,
At reading fortunes, and that he wad fpae
Mine tightly to me, ere that he fud gae,
For, in my face, he faid, he clearly faw,
Some lucky turn was nae juft far awa.

Syn'

S, a taul' me mony things he brawly kent,

Ard wi' the rest gae me this wyly hint,

That, gin I did dra Bess's friend discard,

I adone, wi th gem Bess, lose the Land

Dcn But wast a, was it, Helen can ye tell,

Tu tr covered as the lad himsell?

When he was fae disguis'd a' round about,

I fest lo ee e fin' at out

H Then gae'n me d m ic'd to hit a Letter fi',

W ont me ken, t ms young strong-fi'.

Syn I directi gae doot to d' the Knight,

The ad said e to arrange right

d the for e he afore,

D g w Bess ght in the door;

A t rea he ee fee,

Fett g lt to h un th t to me,

T e e e d ght trace,

Or me round u t upon the case

S row p s out gin ye'll hep her,

I'll, ma le gme of lest explain.

A se gae d lo r best ale,

e e r ce l a'ed re my tale.

                         [*Exeunt.*

                                     ACT

ACT V. SCENE I.

PROLOGUE TO THE SCENE

The Knight's large Ha,
A' round the ...,
In rightest ... dr...,
... g... Forbears,
... two ... years,
Th... ... ...
... ...,
... ...,
And, s... ... to share,
In his strange ...,
To raise ... N... k,
And give Ned a share

Kn SUCH base reproaches, it were hard to bear,
 Which must to Innocence give pain to hear,
And from whatever cause it may proceed,
Nought can excuse the blackness of the deed
Whoe'er the conduct of the Fair would stain,
Should be excluded from the rank of men
Whose duty 'tis, to guard their weaker form,
From every danger, and vile threat'ning harm
And 'tis his honour, and his duty too,
To give such wretches up to contempt ...,
Who daring, thus, fair Woman to defame,
Prove foes to Virtue and their Sex's fame.

What

What art I ha e, that art I mean to try,
And hope to fhow the author of this lie,
But, it were better, that he had reveal'd
This of himfelf, which canna be conceal'd.
For I fhall, quickly, make fome ane appear,
Wha will the ftory, in a hurry, clear.
But what's the matter, Ned, ye tremble fae ?

Ned. God blifs your Honour, gin ve'd lat me ga'e !
Gin ye fud raife the De'il, ere I depart,
I'm very fear the fight will flit my heart!
I never fall do guid ahin the fright,
Gin I be forc'd to bide the ugfome fight!

Kn. He'll get nae pow'r but o'er the guilty mind,
For a' befide, will to the fight be blind

Hel. Gin Ned has dane nae ill, he needfna fear,
Tho' a' the De'ils in Hell fud now appear.

Ned Ay, ay, nae doubt, but wha cud be fae baul,
As fay he ne'er did ought to harm his faul ?
I ha'e my fau'ts, there's few can fay they're free,
And hinna err'd, fometimes, as well as me !

Kn That a' are finners, Ned, we maun agree.
Nor, is our charity fae freely fma',
As think that ye're the greateft of us a'.
Ye needna fear, ye have nae caufe of dread,
Unlefs ye have been guilty of this deed.
A' other fauts will pafs unrotic'd now,
But he, wha has done this, may chance to rue

Nane

Nane here maun ſtir, but let my ſpell proceed,
On names of fame I call, and folks lang deid.

Great Don Quixote De La Mancha,
With thy truſty Sancho Pancha !
Quick, my ſummons now obey,
And ſeek thoſe ſcenes excluding day,
Where conſtant night, and horror dwells,
And guilty ſon's, in burning cells,
Forever on their torments cry,
Gnaw'd by the worm which ne'er will die !
Where gnaſhing teeth, and endleſs weeping,
Prevent the ſufferers from ſleeping,
And feeling ſtill increaſe of pain,
Grin deep, and clank their burning chains !
Where Pluto, on his fiery throne,
With proud, pleaſure mocks each groan,
Drawing freſh torments from his eyes,
Whilſt, round him, flames ſulphureous riſe,
By which, to every guilty ſhade,
Increaſe of torture is convey'd ;   }
And, o'er the gloom, millions, greater   }
            horror ſpread !

Go, mighty Don, and quickly bring,
To Earth, that condemned King !
And, for his trouble, he ſhall have,
The wretches a perpetual ſlave,
Who, during ſuch baſe here to tell,
Betrays a friend ſtraight for Hell !

                                        [S. N. TO LY.

L

I find my call has reach'd his ear,
And, soon, h s Highne's will appeal !
These flames declare he is at hand,
And, thus, I g ve him the command !
ALD BARON TIP HOSCOP HORN IO FLY,
Seize, as thy prey, the author of this lie?

> *Bra—y, — a, al' bad o' Ned,*
> *Juf li' so fa' for fear,*
> *W en, is crie to the Knight to red*
> *Thi-k-g the D 'il o'er near*

Ned. Help, help, I find he has me in his claws,
Oh, r m, 'ay h m. fir, for ony's caufe,
And I'll confess, and play fie tricks nae mair.

Bra. I trow, friend Ned, your heart has got a fkare

Geo Gin he's the author of this lie, De'il care·

Ki. Are ye the man ! It's well ye taul' in time,
Elfe ye had fuffer d deeply for the crime.
But, as t's in my po'r, I row prevent
The fate cifrv'd, and hope ye w 'l repent.

> S n e re to trades u n ght,
> S nce all, w tho t vou a d, is right.

Geo. That so e kind—but tho' l e pass e en now,
The De'il ill get him yet, or tyn his due.

He. Keep ye your claws, ye rattle-headed ass,
It's nae your p t fie sentences to pass.
Gin ye, to Befs, had had a heart la fu 1,
To trow fie tricks, ye ne'er had been fo fu',
Ye fid be pun f' , t a fa — a — ,

Geo. I own my fau't, but gin she will forgi'e,
I'll tak' her by the hand afore the Priest,
And ne'er again sall be so big a beast

Kn I fear that offer, George, now winna do,
But I sud leave the answer, Bess, to you

Hel For a' my love, ere sic a thing sud be,
Her, in her winding sheet, I'd rather see.

Bess Gin that's your mind, we winna disagree
I freely can forgi'e him the offence,
But when I wed, I'll wed a lad o sense.

Kn That's rightly said—George, ye are much to
And well deserve to lose your former claim. (blame,
Ne'er trust a tale, which envious tongues may raise,
Or credit ought that's to a lass disprai e
But let this loss, in future, make you wise.

Geo And sae it may, I've tint o'er guid a prize
Wae to you Ned, I will repent it ay,
I lootna Simon brak your banes the day
To gar me think ye was my dearest friend,
And be at heart my foe, when a' was done

Ned O Geordy, Geordy—am I really here !

Geo I'm wae ye are, ye base confounded liar

Ned Am I alive, and do I see you yet !

Geo Ay, and sud fin me too, gin I durst let

Kn Beware of that, tho' there were no redress
Or else your folly ye may yet repent.
I'll judge if farther punishment be fit,
Gin Edward anes had gather'd a' his wits

And yet I'm sure I'll never, a' my life,
Confide in ought, tho' I had want a wife.
O fir, forgive I' and nae war defign,
But, by the tither, to ftrive to mak' her mine.
And tho' I uf'd, wi rudenefs, your good name,
I fwear my word cud never hurt your fame :
But thought your goodnefs, gin it fud fucceed,
Wad pardon me the bafenefs of the deed.

Kn. How cud you think, to 'fcape the vengeance due,
Or that fuch crimes cud be conceal'd from view ?
Thro' Love's and Friendfhip's ftricteft ties to brake,
Muft the juft wrath of Providence awake:
Who, wifely, brings fuch wickednefs to light,
To make us look, with horror, on the fight ;
And fhow fuch deeds, tho' hid to us they ly,
Are ne'er conceal'd from his all-feeing eye !
Lovar', your fault is of no common kind,
And fhows a ftrange depravity of mind.
The 'fcape, you've made, is mair than ye deferve,
But let it as a warning to you ferve :
And ne'er, again, provoke the wrath of Heaven,
And ye may hope, this anes, to be forgiven.
Let honefty your fma'eft actions guide,
And, aboon a', in Love it fhould prefide.

Ivel. O fir, as lang's I ever live or breathe,
I ne'er falldo a living creature fkath !

Kn.

Kn Well, be it fo —the part fha'l, be forgot,
And, Befs, I hope, ye now forgive the plot?

Befs Wi' a' my heart —proud, in my humble ftate,
To follow the example which ye fet.

Geo. I'm fcar tho' Befs, ye never will agree
To marry Ned, when ye have flighted me!

Befs. Gin that can pleafe, alike I flight you baith,
To wed with either, I'd be very laith.

Omnes. There's few, wethink, can blame you fair for
Baith ha'e been guilty of o'er grite a fau't.   [that;

Era But, there's a lad, that I wad fain propofe,
I hope mair worthy o' her love than thofe,
Nor do I think, gin I hae ony guefs,
She'll tak' my offer ony way annifs.
What fay you, Befs? How wad ye like my friend?

Kn. Is this your Nephew, Branky, that ye mean?

Bra. The fame, an' like your Honour to approve;
Wi' Befs, he's freely o'er the lugs in love.
Since e'er he faw her, he nae reit can find,
Nor is fhe ever abfent frae his mind.
'Bout naething ither maift he thinks or fpeaks,
But making ballats on her rofy cheeks,
Her fparkling een, or her faft flowing hair,
And fwears nae face was ever ha'f fo fair.
A' day he cracks about her in this ftrain,
And fyn, at night, dreams a'thing o'er again.
And gin fhe difna bear him fome regard,
I'll fay the love, atween them, is ill fhar'd.

Kn.

Kn T me, whofe he rt, ith fo much warmnefs
It wad be hard, gin fhe a pity fhows   (glows,
I hope the breafts with equal wifhes burn,
Such love, I think, deferves to meet return

Pra. I think your Honour, that was kindly faid.

Kn. Befs dinna blufh, but fpeak, nor be afraid.
If he's agreeable, ye needna fear,
To lat the love, he merits now appear
Yet, tho' I think ye canna well defpife,
Let Love alane direct you in the choice.
My thoughts I only mention, as a friend,
I woud be nane, fhould I to more pretend.
It is your right, and now fhou'd be your part,
To liften to the dictates of your heart.

Befs. Encouraged by your Honour, ever kind,
It 's my duty to declare my mind,
Nor of the lad need I think ony fhame,
Or blufh to own I feel an honeft flame.

Bra. That fpeech mith claw the billy's back I'm fear,
I wonder he's fae lang o' coming here.

Kn. I think I bade you bring the lad alang—

Bra. I taul' him, fir, but then he wadna gang
He is fae nice, and ay maun be fo fprufh ,
That he ran hame to gi'e his claes a brufh.
He faid he cudna think to fee the Knight,
'Till he fud mak' himfell mair fnod and tight.
But he'll be here, I'm fear he wadna bide,
Gin he but kent what's likely to betide.

                         But

But what, now, to the match does Helen say?
We cudna just agree upon't, the day

Bess Naething seems wanting, but her kind consent,
To blifs my choice, and gi'e me full content.

Hel I'm sorry, then, that I maun difapprove
Of ine, for whom ye feem to bear fic love.
Nor can I now, without fincere regrete,
Seek to oppofe the feem ng will of Fate.
But, for the beft of reafons, I deny,
Nor, wi' that bargain, think I'll e'er comply.
The lad, tho' guid enough, maun better be,
Ere I can freely to the match agree

Bess I thought it mair than ye'd expect to me.
I ftrange to hear ye fpeak in fic a ftile,
Gin ye can be in earneft a the while.

Hel. To a', nae doubt, who now are ftanding here,
My conduct may, in fic ftrange light appear.
Nor do I wonder they, as well as you,
Sud o this matter ha'e the fame falfe view;
And think what diff'rence, they are fit to fpy,
Can, only, in tnis youngman's favour, ly.
But better than they a' I ken your worth.

Bef. I'm neither rich, nor yet o' gentle birth.
Speak out, and eaf my breaft of anxious pain

K1 Helen, it's fair ye make your reafons plain.
Whate'er they be, it's fit they get a name,
Ere either party quit fae guid a claim.

Hel. That fhe's nae rich is fure o'er true, indeed,
But it's as true, fhe is of gentle blood.

And

And, w... gea... ... ... Lad,

P... ...ns ... ...ed w... ...r'd

Dea Aunt I... ... ...u lute!

Kn Ha... ...no wishes, ... to be grite?

Bess I ... ...ned our wishes, sir so vain,

Nore ... ... my humble lot complain.

S ... ...d of happiness pa ... ...e,

I ... ...n I've been my with end make,

L ... ... jamie, he s my only care,

For him ... ... I wish, and n ...thing mair.

And were e'en grandeur new with in my pow'r,

So that a wish cud the rich prize secure,

If, on the change, wi' Jamie I loot part,

I'd tare the thought, wi' pleasure, frae my heart.

JAMIE enters in his own Character of SETON-HA',
in a hurt'ng dress.

Seton In me, behold that happy youth, sweet maid,
Who heard, with rapture, a' ye've kindly said.
I hope you winna love your Jamie less,
Tho' he has now put on a former dress
Ye ll now remind the happy show'r of rain,
And what I promis'd, should we meet again.
Aunty, I hope now, winna disagree,
And what ye arena, ye shall sortly be.

Bess. I have nae words——

Dor ——————————I fear the lass will swoon!

Bess. Some ane support me! or I kurap dead down!

Seton.

Set. That charge become—here, on my bosom, lean·
No sweeter armful was ever hold
While this I press thee, and ten thousand charms,
I fold a Paradise within my arms!
This tempeft of the foul will foon wear o'er,
And Beffy fmile, and blifs me, as before.

   Bess Fain wad I fpeak, but kenna what to fay,
This blifs furprize bears a' my fenfe away.

   Seton Look on thy Jamie, and compofe thy mind,

   Bess I fee, I fee, none elfe cud be fo kind!
I darena doubt, and yet I fomething fear

   Seton There is no caufe I hope, when he's fo near.

   Bess. Delightfu' man—can ane fo highly born,
Look upon me, and yet nae look wi' fcorn!

   Seton. What eye could fcorn, that half thy charms
What heart but muft to fo much beauty yield! [beheld!
Nor is thy form polluted by thy mind,
For both alike are matchlefs and refin'd!

   Bess I thought my Jamie ay o'er gud for me·

   Seton In that alane, may we ay difagree.
How will fuch fweetnefs fmooth the cares of life,
When I'm fo happy as can call thee wife!

   Bess. Too generous man! ye force my hopes to rife!
O that the World cud but approve your choice!
O that my Aunty's tale had been but true,
Tho' nought cud ever make me merit you!
But, if that love can anfwer for a name,
Your happinefs fhall be my conftant aim

                         Bel.

J. Ye mcclu . . . . , . I ha'e to . . nae he,

. . . for ch . . . . horn . s he

J. . . I'den . . ke . . . . 'out' at fire . . . ra be.

J. An' I . . . . ar Honor, . . . at, it's very true,

Tho' . . . . tie, I ne'er toul' this to you.

I . . , . . I e'er had . . . ded it wi' ane,

I . . had been . ou, who . . was sic a friend

I hope sic'll nae be thought less worth his love,

That I can Bess his blood-relation prove.

An' had the Sun that raise . . . shone as fair,

. . en th ha'e been mair worthy o' his care

. . . . . speak, Helen, speak whate'er ye ha'e to say;

For we can credit ony thing the day!

Seton. Ay speak, and quickly, I'm in pain to hear:

Hel. Whate'er I say, this Writing will make clear.

{ *Taking a Letter from her*
{ *bosom and giving to Seton-ha.*

Tho' clouds ha'e lang obscur'd her hapless fate,

Ye but enjoy what sud be her Estate.

I at never ane 'gainst Providence complain,

Since she, anes mair, is like to get her ain.

Seton. Good Heaven! the name my hapless Cousin

Oft, have I wept at his hard fate before!   (bore!

Part of your tale I do already ken,

And what I dinna, hope ye can explain.

Shall I, as on his daughter, look on Bess?

Hel. Ye may, for I can prove she is nae less.

Seton.

Seton As fuch, let me embrace he, th'...

Tho' nought can make thee dearer ...
  Once been, grown, we ... yet ...
  S on How come ye here? ke no ...
  Pal That ye fha'll en, but ... I cann ...
What ane, except yourfell, that s ...
Her Father fud ha'e been ...
But that his pride was hurt by a ...
So as the p... was not like to be,
'Cafe he h d wea'ed, and his defire,
A lofs of heart, and of ... w th,
In... to ane, except rich
Yet a' ... for the ...
Had, tint... and dead h, ... been,
Which happen d foon, o time ...
And, in his ... , t ...
To your broke his ... , then d... ,
An la'th a lover ...
A' now was dark, the ...
And but h f ...
At laft refolv'd, to fore ...
To feek that fortune, ...
And left, ... de ...
His ... fe and D is to ...
Unkent to ..., and in ...
Ae might I ...

A . . . . last wife,

. . . . life

. . . . cast,

. . . .

. . . . that knew it was a . . .,

. . . . the . . . f . . . . and me.

D . Av . . . 's that tale, for till this very day,

I . . r k . . . . fay !

. . . . What then befell the Mother ? hapless fair !

. . . . me she spent some years of grief and care;

I . . . . nothing from the youth she lov'd,

. . . . s o'er heavy for her prov'd;

S . . . . child, then smil'd and welcom'd death,

. . . . yielded up her latest breath,

. . . . 'd . . . . closest secrecy to keep,

A . . . . t the story, in my bosom, sleep;

' . . . Fortune, f it ever was so kind,

S . . . d . . . . her child, anes mair, a Father find.

S . . . t . . . . . t, that sud he ne'er return again,

' . . . . her birth, with only gi'e her pain ;

. . . . . her murmur at the lot decreed,

L . . . . . w, the tale may help to raise her head.

B . Tho' great my loss, that loss I never knew,

T . . want so kindly was supplied by you.   (aid,

. . . . . I was kind, indeed, to gi'e such generous

A . . I . . . . hope to see you well repaid.

[To Helen.
Whatever

Whatever life attends me and the Fair,
With us ye'll live, and kindly take a share.
And Branky, you, who aye have stood my friend,
Maun as our frequent visitant be seen.
Simon and Kattie too, I must regard,
And, at a proper season, will reward.
A double wedding we shall shortly ha'e,
And baith receive our Beauties on one day.
Where, a' now here, maun on our joys attend,
And ilk ane be made welcome as a friend.

 Kn. And ye'll allow that I fit out the Bride,
And stand, that day, as Father by her side.
When, tho' nae dow'r such beauty seems to want,
I well can spare, and will, with pleasure, grant
Such little present, as some use may fair,
And show my approbation of the pair.

 Seton. Words are too weak to tell how much we owe,
Such goodness ne'er can meet reward below !

 Kn. My full reward will in the pleasure ly

 Seton. I ll say no more, such kindness mocks reply!

 Hel. As ye've sae kindly credited the past,
Of a' my ferlies, hear the greatest last.
My lang lost foster-bairn I'll shortly see,
And Bessy, in a Father, happy be ;
Who will ilk friend, in a fit manner, thank,
And gi'e her fortune equal to her rank.

 Omnes. Can it be possible what now we hear !

       [*Holding up their eyes.*

         Hel.

Ha! Thank God! the happy truth will soon appear!
If ye a witness of the truth demand,
I hope I'll shortly ha'e him at your hand
As I came here, the news were brought to me,
And made me just as blith as blith cud be
This day, he landed safe, at Aberdeen,
And, by my elder Brother, he was seen
Who came, express, the happy news to tell,
And this he, surely, was me here himsell
This night he bade me look for his approach,
Attended by black servants, in a coach

H—— hasta say to tell me on that,
F—— r'd his slofs and his abid man,
Te—— to meet him, and come to far a here,
And, as I come, I here, the welcome now
T—— her, I fmo 'tem perrwithim breast,
Cast—— e he—— d h his's cond id he first

S—— Sm——, fare man, and let us yet em-
Is th—— that ger—— p——e—— th—— p——ace

B—— I—— dous h——d! I said Far——d,
F—— re—— d thr too, too gene——us mind!
H—— by —— at, h—— sh a Mother's vo,
I—— —— r—— t, —— f ree ater to find

A—— Le—— —— al, er forro—— no ate o'er,
And Te——s —— lng em——— wo——d her peace no more
Mo——er he—— e, which am on Earth—— ed,
In p——d th—— s is love, —— hea'n, sup——

                                    Whate'er

Whate'er befalls, let a'l still put their trust,
In Him, whose ways, tho' dark, are ever just!
A truth this day's occurrence serves to prove,
In this strange instance of your happy love!

Seton. Happy indeed!—

Omnes ——————————Lang may your joys last,
And ilka day prove happier than the past!

S A N G   XII

Tune —*Etrick Banks*

H E L E N.

MY no remembrance of the past,
The rising buds of pleasure blast,
But purest bliss attend the Pair,
Uncircular'd with the gall of care!

S E T O N

Soon as the nuptial knot is tied,
Let ev'ry painful thought subside,

B E S S

May this blyth night our sorows end,
And Fortun, henceforth, prove our friend!

K N I G H T

May ev'ry gen'rous lover find
His darling fair, like Peggy, kind,
And ever meet the due reward,
Or un-interested and pure regard!

OMNES,

JAMIE AND BESS.

O N E S.

What heart! but will, with rapture, join
To supplicate the Power Divine!
Which sends such blessings from above,
As the reward of gen'rous love.

[*Exeunt Omnes.*

They now retire, yet as the curtain fa',
And as ye've, kind, stay'd the end of a',
I gi'e you thanks, and leave, now, to withdraw.

THE END.

DE AE

EPILOGUE.

Written by Mr SUTHERLAND.

And spoken by Mrs HAMILTON.

ALL trembling and shaking within sits the Bard,
Who waits with impatience your fate's award,
On his *Pegasus* mounted, he ambled along,
In pastoral verse, and melodious song,
His thoughts all employ'd on his *Jamie and Bess*,
And conceiving the transport he'd crown'd with success,
But alas! if a task'd on his humour, dismay'd,
He should find his young *Peg* prove a ticklish jade,
And tumble poor author clean down in the dirt,
Remember, he's lame, and may easy get hurt
Consider his case then, and his fall is near on,
You see he's got his foot fixed into the stirrup,
Reverse but the scene, send your surmise abroad,
He'll pleasantly amble, your smiles cheer the road,
'Tho' numbe his professions, he seems to' not in 5,
You'll hear him sing well both o' you and I scratch,
Oh! give him your plaudits, the joy, 'twill afford,
Must be past expression—*y with Bon Accord*

* The Aberdeen Motto.

After the Epilogue, the following *Address to his Crutch* was
sung by Mrs HAMILTON.

BLYTH days I have seen,
Gl rad they fti'l been,
I ne'erwould have ma'ea compan on of the,
Au fince they are gane,
It is vain to reer pain,
We're wedded, I fear, and had beft now agree!

Au met oas the nyd,
The ast of sunds,
Employ ng Glears, chupa d remit er tee,
They ccwle en coms,
A us, frasro goo,
And tho art le sail deher ad forme!

III
To bee more lene,
Than any one,
My fa ht s power vherever I pleafe,
V douu dele aud,
A cul o al rue,
And I ave no fretune to keep me at eafe!

IV
Then, ler me embrace thee,
Co ter ec e efetree,
Whaf, t cer rrar, I now prefs thee, thus hine,
Sire i earrct at lef,
E u rtm frietain ferof,
And tha I yur er tear a ry fee!

‡ For te if of h   rifs fe orty Pieces of mufic
titention sodle ght Len a i a Ball or abbon,

GLOSSARY of such uncommon Scotch Words as occur in the Piece.

ABLINS, *maybe, no doubt*
Browdent on the lass, *deeply in love with her*
Bedeen, *directly, instantly or immediately*
Birly, *a term similar to Old-boy*
C l i *Whistle*
Coff *to Buy*
Clack, *saucy discourse*
Curl *gloomy thoughts*
In, *to sit close*
Dree *to suffer*
Etch, *uneasy thing*
Eith, *eithly eas., easily or readily*
Eke, *also*
Forgie, *forgive*
Fluff d or Huffed, *disappointed*
Forgeder *to meet*
Failui *to forsake*
J to *fear or be afraid of*
Fou , *plenty*
Gul- heep or Gul-wleep, *great*
Knap, *a small eminence or fairy*
fle, *feet*
Heal, *conceal*
Jee *o far or remote from its place*
Jee', *to be —*

Hack, *to slight*
Lighthe, *light*
Leisom *warm, sultry.*
Loo'd, *loved*
Mirky *speaking joy, mirthful, pleased*
Mense, *manners*
Queer *strange or curious.*
Pea *to suppose, or guess*
Endle *seldom*
Stoure, *stitch*
Strippin', or strapan, *tall, genteel, handsome*
Sell, *money.*
Snish *snuff*
Smergh, *strength*
Stelly, *ill-naturedly, sharp.*
Sha', to *show*
Stap *to stop or close up.*
Steek, *to shut close*
Tift, *Case or Trim.*
Tyn, *to lose*
Wad, *to wager*
Ween *Suppose*
Wishy-washies *a cant term for lengthened discoursing o the point.*
Winsome, *delightful or agreeable.*
Ye'lly, *you will soon.*

CPSIA information can be obtained
at www.ICGtesting.com
Printed in the USA
BVOW04s0019301117
501329BV00068B/1607/P